AN URBAN INSTITUTE PAPER

EXTERNALITIES, SEGREGATION, AND HOUSING PRICES

Ann Burnet Schnare

208-24

A report on research supported by *Department of Housing and Urban Development Office of Policy Development and Research*

BOARD OF TRUSTEES

Robert S. McNamara, *Chairman*
Jean Fairfax
Eugene G. Fubini
William Gorham
Katharine Graham
Robert V. Hansberger
Vernon E. Jordan, Jr.
Edward Hirsch Levi
Richard Llewelyn-Davies
Bayless A. Manning
Stanley Marcus

Arjay Miller
J. Irwin Miller
Franklin D. Murphy
John D. Rockefeller IV
Herbert Scarf
Charles L. Schultze
William W. Scranton, *Vice-Chairman*
Franklin A. Thomas
Cyrus R. Vance
John G. Veneman
James Vorenberg

INSTITUTE OFFICERS

William Gorham, *President*
Robert Harris, *Senior Vice-President*
Harold W. Guthrie, *Vice-President for Research*
Herman T. Boland, Jr., *Vice-President for Administration*
Edward E. Wallace, *Controller*

The Urban Institute is a nonprofit research corporation established in 1968 to study problems of the nation's urban communities. Independent and nonpartisan, the Institute responds to current needs for disinterested analyses and basic information and attempts to facilitate the application of this knowledge. As part of this effort, it cooperates with federal agencies, states, cities, associations of public officials, the academic community and other sectors of the general public.

The Institute's research findings and a broad range of interpretive viewpoints are published as an educational service. Conclusions expressed in Institute publications are those of the authors and do not necessarily reflect the views of other staff members, officers or trustees of the Institute, or of organizations which provide funds toward support of Institute studies.

These research findings are made available in three series of publications: Books and Reports, Papers, and Reprints. A current publications list is available on request.

Publications Office

The Urban Institute
2100 M Street, N.W.
Washington, D.C. 20037

EXTERNALITIES, SEGREGATION, AND HOUSING PRICES

Ann Burnet Schnare

208-24

July 1974

THE URBAN INSTITUTE
WASHINGTON, D.C.

Soc
HD
7287.5
S34

The research forming the basis for this study was funded in part by the Office of Policy Development and Research, U.S. Department of Housing and Urban Development. Opinions expressed are those of the author and do not necessarily represent the views of The Urban Institute or its sponsors.

LIBRARY
FLORIDA STATE UNIVERSITY
TALLAHASSEE, FLORIDA

NOV 24 1975

UI 208-24
ISBN 87766-046-8

REFER TO URI-28000 WHEN ORDERING.

Available from:

Publications Office
The Urban Institute
2100 M Street, N.W.
Washington, D.C. 20037

List price: $2.50

A/74/300

ABSTRACT

This study presents a theoretical and an empirical analysis of the relationship between housing prices and the ethnic, racial, and socio-economic composition of a dwelling unit's neighborhood.

The theoretical section of the paper develops a simple, long-run equilibrium model of household location that relates demographic externalities to housing market segregation and to intra-metropolitan rent and value differentials.

The remainder of the study attempts to verify some of the implications of that model. In particular, it examines the relationship in Boston between housing prices and a neighborhood's concentration of black, Italian, Puerto Rican, and Chinese households. By estimating the differentials that were associated with concentrations of each of these four groups in both 1960 and 1970, and by relating the observed changes in those premiums to changes in the groups' overall growth and composition, this study attempts to isolate the price effects of demographic externalities.

ACKNOWLEDGMENTS

This paper is a condensed version of <u>An Empirical Analysis of the Dimensions of Neighborhood Quality</u> (unpublished Ph.D. dissertation, Harvard University, 1974).

Frank de Leeuw devised the study's two-tiered estimating technique and provided valuable aid throughout its preparation.

My two thesis advisors, John F. Kain and Gregory Ingram, helped formulate many of the basic concepts embodied in the paper.

Raymond J. Struyk and Sue Marshall read earlier drafts with care and suggested ways of improving the analysis.

The U.S. Department of Housing and Urban Development, through The Urban Institute, funded much of the statistical analysis.

CONTENTS

	Page
Abstract	iii
Acknowledgment	v
I. Introduction	1
II. Demographic Externalities, Segregation, and Housing Prices	3
III. Methodology	13
IV. The 1970 Regressions	17
A. The 1970 Stage I Regressions	18
B. The 1970 Stage II Regressions	26
V. A Comparison of the 1960 and 1970 Stage II Regressions	41
A. Parameter Bias in the Revised Stage II Equations	43
B. Differentials in the Estimated Parameters	50
VI. Conclusion	59
Appendices	63

List of Tables

1.	The 1970 Stage I Regressions	22
2.	The 1970 Stage II Regressions	28
3.	The 1970 Ethnic and Racial Price Differentials	31
4.	The Distribution of Neighborhood Attributes by Bundle Size in the 1970 Sample	42
5.	A Comparison of the 1970 Stage II Coefficients obtained with Different Stage I Neighborhood Variables	48
6.	A Comparison of the Coefficients Obtained in the 1970 Tenure-Specific and Combined Regressions	47
7.	A Comparison of the 1960 and the 1970 Stage II Regressions	51

I. Introduction

This study presents a theoretical and an empirical analysis of the relationship between housing prices and the ethnic, racial, and socio-economic composition of a dwelling unit's neighborhood. Externalities induced by a wide-spread aversion or attraction to certain kinds of neighbors may influence the location decisions of households and may thereby affect the city's structure of housing rents and values. Although the early literature on the social stratification and the structure of urban areas emphasized the importance of these demographic variables, recent urban economists, seemingly infatuated with the concept of an accessibility-rent tradeoff, having generally ignored their role. This study attempts to integrate these two bodies of literature by constructing an economic model of interdependent household location decisions and by empirically estimating some of its implications pertaining to the intrametropolitan variation of housing prices.

The theoretical section of this paper develops a simple, long-run equilibrium model of household location which examines the relationship between externalities, housing market segregation, and housing prices. Under assumption of perfectly mobile households and complete supply adjustment, externalities will normally produce highly segregated neighborhoods with rent differentials that reflect the demographic preferences of their residents.

The remainder of the study attempts to verify some of the implications of this equilibrium model of household behavior. In particular, it examines the relationship in Boston between housing rents and values and a neighborhood's concentration of black, Italian, Puerto Rican, and Chinese households. By estimating the differentials that were associated with concentrations of each of these four groups in both 1960 and 1970, and by relating the observed changes in these premiums to changes in the groups' overall growth and composition, this study attempts to isolate the price effects of demographic externalities.

The basic assumption underlying our empirical analysis is that the rent (or value) of a given dwelling unit depends on the characteristics of the unit, $\{X\}$, and of its neighborhood, $\{N\}$, so that:

$$R = R(X, N)$$

Under this assumption, a regression of rent (R) on $\{X\}$ and $\{N\}$ will yield estimates of the implicit market prices of the various housing attributes. The resulting "hedonic price equation" is a common tool of housing market analyses and, when properly used, can identify those components of the housing bundle that contribute to market values.[1]

This paper presents two such equations for rents and housing values in the Boston metropolitan area, one for 1960 and one for 1970. Each of them is derived from a two-staged procedure, using two distinct data sets: census tract statistics and the One-in-a-Hundred Public Use Sample. The first stage of the analysis is a regression of rent on the structural characteristics of the dwelling unit, employing micro data drawn from the Public Use Sample. The effects of neighborhood are subsumed in the constant: since

---

[1] For a general discussion of this technique, see Zvi Griliches, ed., Price Indices and Quality Change, (Harvard University Press, 1971).

the sample is random, the estimated regression equation describes rents associated with units in an average neighborhood at an average distance from the center of the metropolis. Stage II begins by using this equation to predict an average rent for each census tract in the Boston SMSA, based on the structural characteristics of the dwelling units contained in the tract. Assuming that the tract represents a fairly homogeneous neighborhood, the difference between the actual and this predicted tract rent should depend on the characteristics of the tract itself. Thus, the final step of the analysis is a regression of the calculated tract residuals on the various neighborhood attributes. Although this study concentrates on the influence of the neighborhood's demographic composition, it also estimates the price effects of other important variables included in $\{N\}$ and $\{X\}$.

Following this introduction, the study is in five basic parts: Section 2 contains a general discussion of the theoretical impact of demographic externalities on the location decisions of households and on the structure of housing prices within a metropolitan area; Section 3 describes the estimating technique employed by this study and analyzes some of the statistical problems inherent in its two-tiered approach; Section 4 presents the Stage I and Stage II regressions estimated from the 1970 data set; Section 5 compares the 1970 Stage II neighborhood parameters to similar coefficients derived from the 1960 sample; and Section 6 summarizes the major findings of the study and assesses its implications for future research on the intra-metropolitan variation of housing prices.

II. Demographic Externalities, Segregation, and Housing Prices

The relationship between rent and the demographic characteristics of the neighborhood has generally been ignored in econometric studies of the housing market. Although racial discrimination has been a popular subject, little attention has been paid to the possible effects of other forms of group interaction. Externalities arise when a household's satisfaction depends on the characteristics of its neighborhood; demographic externalities refer to the influence of the demographic mix of an area on a household's evaluation of neighborhood quality. Where such effects are important, they will induce price differentials between otherwise comparable housing bundles.[2] In equilibrium--that is, in a situation where no household has any inducement to move--units in more desirable neighborhoods will rent or sell at a premium. The distinguishing feature of these externalities is that the equilibrium price differentials must satisfy all households, including those who may be regarded as inferior neighbors. Often, incompatible demands can produce extreme patterns of segregation.

The impact of demographic externalities on the location decisions of households and on the structure of housing prices can be illustrated with a simple model of the housing market. Suppose that households fall into two mutually exclusive and exhaustive groups--whites (W) and blacks (B)-- and that members of each of these groups have similar incomes and tastes. The city consists of a number of well defined neighborhoods, or zones, which contain standardized dwelling units and which differ only in their concentration of blacks. For simplicity, we assume that a household's utility is a function of the demographic mix of its zone of residence, and does not depend

---

[2] Martin Bailey, "Effects of Race and Other Demographic Factors on Values of Single-Family Homes," Land Economics, Vol. XLII (May, 1966) pp. 215-220.

on the distribution of households within that zone or on the mix of households of neighboring zones. Assuming that blacks and whites are perfectly mobile, the demographic preferences of the two groups will ultimately be revealed in the intra-metropolitan variation of housing prices.

Some of the possible patterns of demographic preferences are:

1. INDIFFERENCE: Members of both "W" and "B" are indifferent to living with other members of "W" or "B".

2. ONE-SIDED EXTERNALITY: Members of "W" prefer living with other members of the "W" but members of "B" are indifferent to living with other members of "B".

3. TWO-SIDED EXTERNALITY: Members of both "W" and "B" prefer living with members of "W".

4. A PREFERENCE FOR HOMOGENEITY: Members of "W" prefer living with other members of "W", and members of "B" prefer living with other members of "B".

5. PREFERENCE FOR DIVERSITY: Members of both groups prefer living in integrated neighborhoods, although their ideal ratio of "W's" to "B's" may differ.

The equilibrium relationship between housing prices and a zone's proportion of blacks will vary under each of these five alternatives. If blacks and whites are indifferent towards the demographic mix of their neighborhoods, prices in the various zones will be equal, since any differentials that might arise will induce movements out of the high priced zones and into the low priced zones until the discrepancies are eventually eliminated. However, demographic externalities will destroy this equalization of housing prices, and units in preferred areas will rent or sell at a premium.

If both groups preferred living near whites and if prices were originally constant throughout the city, households would move into areas containing low concentrations of blacks. Rents would rise in the predominantly white zones and fall in the predominantly black zones. This movement would alter the demographic mix of zones, which would lead to further adjustment in prices and further inter-zonal movement.

Equilibrium requires that rents fall with a **neighborhood's concentration of blacks**. Initially, new construction in neighborhoods with a favorable demographic mix will narrow these inter-zonal differentials. The increased supply of housing will tend to reduce the premiums received by the area's landlords; as prices fall, additional households will be attracted to the zone. However, the increased competition for vacant land in the predominantly white zones will drive up its price to a level that compensates for its differential earning power. In equilibrium, the price gradient of land will mirror the rent gradient, and returns to builders will be the same in all neighborhoods.

Using similar reasoning, one can determine the equilibrium relationship between rent and the zone's concentration of blacks under each of the remaining hypotheses. Figure 1 illustrates three possible outcomes: with one- or two-sided externalities, rents rise steadily with the proportion of whites; if whites prefer living with whites and blacks prefer living with blacks, the relationship is u-shaped; and if both groups prefer integrated neighborhoods, the differentials resemble an inverted-u. Note that the above model can easily be modified to incorporate variations in other structural and neighborhood attributes of the housing bundle. As long as households are mobile, the rent differentials associated with the various hypotheses regarding household tastes remain the same.

The above analysis can be made more precise by considering the relationship between externalities and the spatial distribution of households. Continuing with our simple model of household location, suppose that members of both groups prefer living in neighborhoods that are predominately white. The two curves depicted in Figure 2.a show the rent differentials required

FIGURE 1

LONG RUN EQUILIBRIUM RENT DIFFERENTIALS
UNDER VARIOUS HYPOTHESES REGARDING HOUSEHOLD TASTES

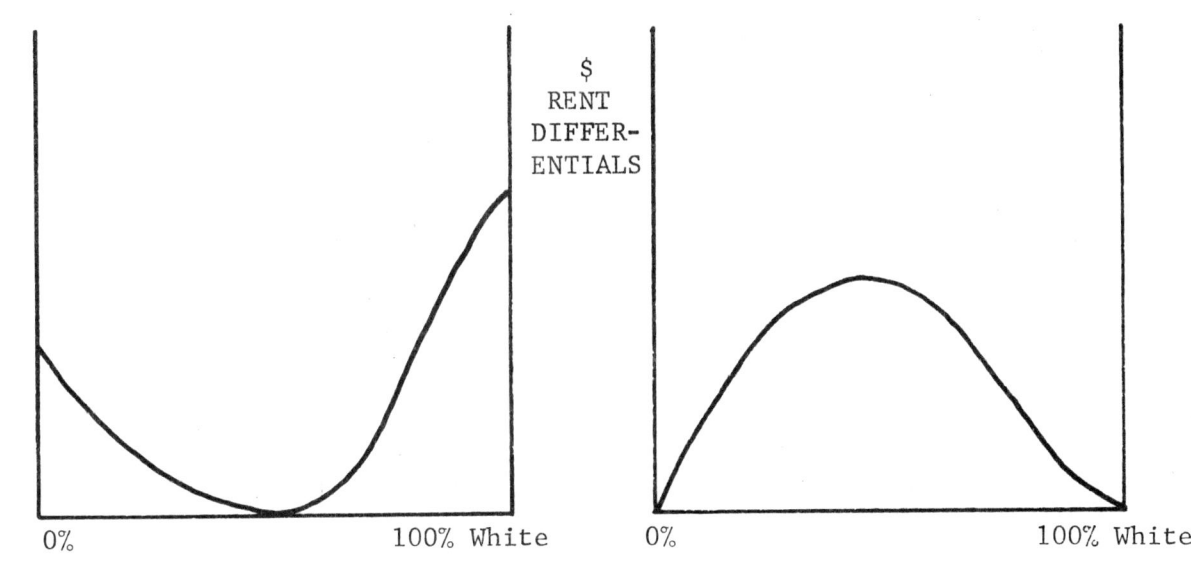

FIGURE 1A: PREFERENCE FOR HOMOGENEITY

FIGURE 1B: PREFERENCE FOR DIVERSITY

FIGURE 1C: ONE OR TWO SIDED EXTERNALITIES

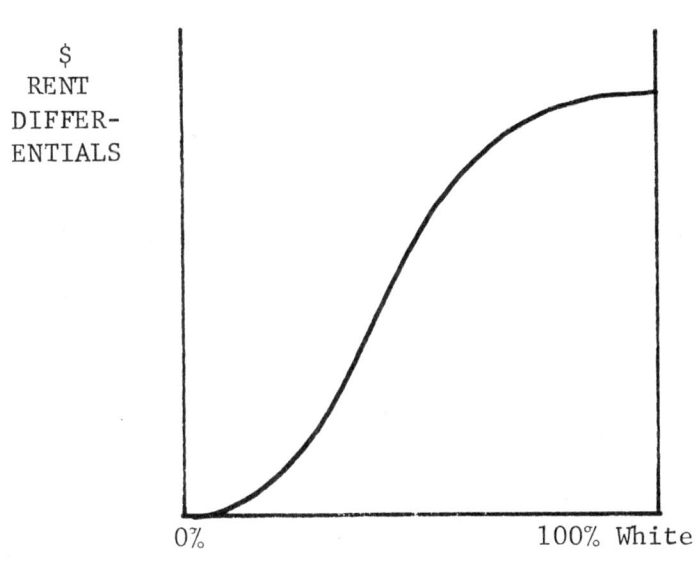

to compensate black and white households for an increased association with blacks; if actual market premiums correspond to "AB" ("AC"), whites (blacks) will be equally well-off in each of the city's zones. Equilibrium requires that both groups be satisfied with the demographic composition of their neighborhoods. If the market differentials originally correspond to the curve "AC", blacks will be willing to live in any of the various zones; a savings in rent just compensates them for their perceived decline in neighborhood quality. Whites, on the other hand, will find integrated neighborhoods distasteful, since the existing market premiums underestimate their preference for living with whites. As they leave these areas in favor of more segregated zones, rising prices in the predominately white neighborhoods will begin to drive out blacks. Eventually, complete segregation will evolve, with prices in the white areas significantly higher than prices in the black areas. No one price structure will satisfy both groups; although blacks and whites rank the various zones in the same order of preference, their demands are incompatible.

In some instances, integrated neighborhoods may exist in equilibrium. Figures 2b and 2c show two situations where the black and the white demand curves intersect. Although both "X" and "Y" are equilibrium positions, only "Y" is stable. A slight shock in the ratio of blacks to whites in Figure 2b would trigger forces that eventually produced a completely segregated zone; an additional white would make the area attractive to both groups, and as prices rose, blacks would be driven out. In contrast, Figure 2c shows a situation where integrated zones are stable; small increases in the proportion of white households would induce inflows of blacks and vice versa. In this instance, a limited amount of integration is consistent with long-run equilibrium.

FIGURE 2-A

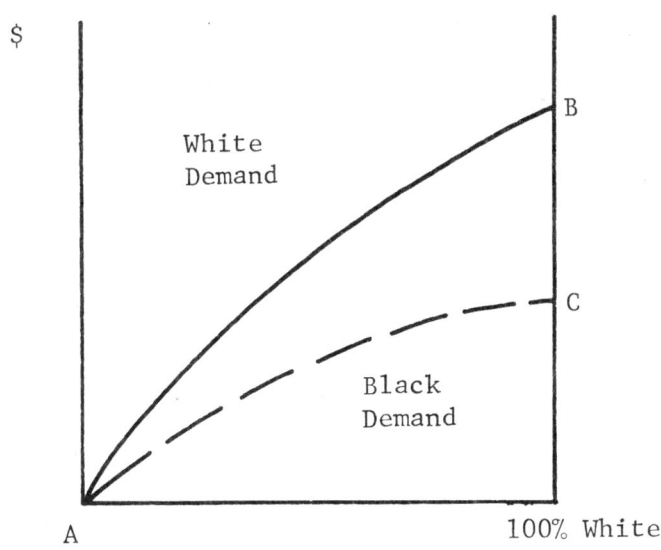

FIGURE 2-B

FIGURE 2-C

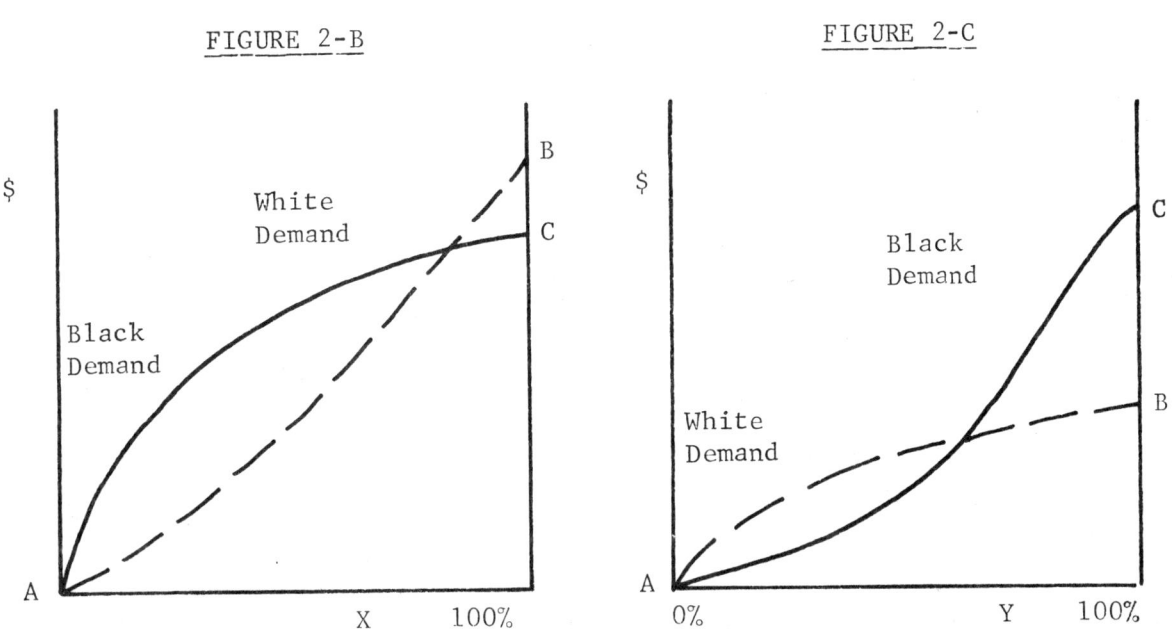

In the above examples, the prospects for integration depend on the slopes of the two income-compensated demand curves, which will increase with: (1) household income and (2) household distaste for living with blacks. If blacks are a minority group, "AC" should lie below "AB" for each type of zone; lower premiums result from lower incomes and weaker preferences for living with whites. In such instances, equilibrium will produce complete segregation. Although both groups prefer living in neighborhoods that are predominantly white, these zones will be too expensive to maintain a stable black population. The situation is similar to an auction: the wealthy buyer with a strong attraction for a particular item will always outbid his opponent.

The prospects for integration seem equally dim when one considers alternative preference patterns. Demand curves may be drawn corresponding to each of the remaining hypotheses regarding household tastes. In most instances, intersection points will represent unstable equilibrium positions. According to this very simple model, integrated neighborhoods (if they exist) will tend to be highly volatile; even if both groups prefer mixed to homogeneous zones, differential incomes combined with differential strengths of preferences will normally prohibit stable bi-racial zones.

To a certain extent, these extreme patterns of segregation reflect the model's assumption of identical intra-group incomes and tastes.[3] With

---

[3] Restrictions to household mobility--such as old age, extreme poverty, or supply constraints--may also encourage a minimal amount of integration by confining families to non-optimal locations. For instance, since school quality tends to be correlated with neighborhood income, good schools will be rare in predominately black zones if the majority of blacks are poor. To obtain a high level of public services, upper income blacks may be forced to reside in neighborhoods containing heavy concentrations of whites. A more equalized income distribution would in this case produce increased segregation.

variable tastes, the curves depicted in Figure 2 become the envelopes of the individual income-compensated demand curves.[4] Normally our conclusions are unaltered. However, if a significant number of blacks and whites are indifferent towards the demographic mix of their neighborhoods, a small number of integrated zones can exist in equilibrium regardless of the majority's preferences. In such instances, households with the highest incomes or the strongest prejudices will live in segregated areas, leaving mixed neighborhoods to households who are unusually poor or unusually liberal. Nevertheless as long as a substantial fraction of one group values the presence of certain kinds of neighbors and as long as most of those households remain relatively mobile, segregation will be fairly pronounced.[5]

The spatial implications of demographic externalities raise the possibility of complete segregation with inter-zonal price equality. In most instances this outcome would be an unstable equilibrium solution, since differentials are normally needed to maintain the status quo and to induce households of both groups to remain in each of their respective neighborhoods; although a range of relative prices may then satisfy the conditions for equilibrium, rents in the two zones will usually differ. However, under the assumptions of our simple model, externalities may in one case fail to induce the predicted pattern of housing rents and values. If whites and blacks are

---

[4] Sherwin Rosen, "Hedonic Prices and Implicit Markets: Product Differentiation in Pure Competition", (unpublished paper).

[5] Thomas Schelling reaches similar conclusions in his various models of segregation, which all ignore the relationship between prices and a households willingness to live with members of a given group. See Thomas Schelling, "A Process of Residential Segregation: Neighborhood Tipping", in Racial Discrimination in Economic Life, Anthony H. Pascal, ed. (Lexington:Lexington Books, D. C. Heath and Co., 1972), and Thomas Schelling, "On the Ecology of Micro-Motives", The Public Interest, No. 25 (Fall, 1971), pp. 59-98.

completely segregated and if both prefer living with members of their own racial or ethnic group, price equality is consistant with household equilibrium.

The indeterminancy of these outcomes stems from the assumed absence of an integrated zone--a condition that is physically impossible unless neighborhoods are separated by artificial or natural barriers. To simplify our analysis, we assumed that a household's utility is constant at all locations within a zone; a more realistic model would relate preferences to proximity, with externalities diminishing with the distance between households. Thus, our attempt to impose fixed boundaries to the various neighborhoods within the city is somewhat misleading, in that it ignores the integration that necessarily exists between two physically contiguous segregated zones.[6] The existence of at least one integrated neighborhood at the boundary restores the one-to-one correspondence between household tastes and market rent differentials. Even with highly segregated neighborhoods, the curves depicted in Figure 1 retain their general validity, although they undoubtedly degenerate into a series of discrete points rather than a continuously defined function.

III. Methodology

The remainder of this study attempts to verify some of the hypotheses presented in the previous section. To identify the major components of neighborhood quality, hedonic price indices are estimated for the Boston SMSA, describing rents (and housing values) in both 1960 and 1970. Our basic model assumes that rents depend on the characteristics of the dwelling unit and its neighborhood, so that:

Eq. 1 $\qquad R_{it} = \sum_j \alpha_j X_{jit} + \sum_k \beta_k N_{kit} + \epsilon_{it}$

---

[6] Bailey's model explicitly explores boundary effects of this sort. (See Martin Bailey, op cit.)

where "R_{it}" is the rent of the "i^{th}" unit in the "t^{th}" tract; $\{X_j\}$ and $\{N_k\}$ are a set of variables describing the structural and the neighborhood attributes of the unit, respectively; and "ϵ_{it}" is a random error which is normally distributed with zero mean and constant variance "s^2". Units in the same census tract are assumed to be in the same neighborhood, so that $N_{kit} = N_{klt}$ for all "i," "l" in "t".

To obtain information on both the structural and the neighborhood attributes of the dwelling unit, it was necessary to combine two distinct data sources, the One-in-a-Hundred Public Use Sample and the Census Tract Reports. The former is a random sample of one percent of the households in the country, classified by state and, in 1970, by urbanized area. Although the Public Use Sample contains a detailed description of the structural attributes of the dwelling unit, its locational and neighborhood data is incomplete in the 1970 sample and virtually non-existent in the 1960 sample. In contrast, tract data from the Census of Population and Housing describes many aspects of neighborhood quality, since it provides information on the tract's resident households and on the average characteristics of its dwelling units.

To combine these micro and macro samples, we adopted a two-staged regression technique, which estimates the "α's" and the "β's" in separate regressions based on the two distinct data sets.[7] A slight manipulation

---

[7] An alternative approach might have relied solely on census tract summary statistics, and regressed average tract rents on the average structural and neighborhood characteristics of the housing bundle. However, the variables appearing in such an equation would undoubtedly be highly collinear, since averaging tends to eliminate most of the independent variation within and between the two classes of attributes. Presumably, this two-staged approach will reduce the variables' multicollinearity, thereby increasing the precision of the regression estimates.

of Equation 1 transforms it into a form more amenable to this procedure:

Eq. 2
$$\left(R_{it} - \sum_j \alpha_j X_{jit}\right) = \sum_k \beta_k N_{kit} + \epsilon_{it}$$

In the first stage of our analysis, rent is regressed on the structural characteristics of the unit, using micro data obtained from the One-in-a-Hundred Public Use Sample. If we replace the "α's" in Equation 2 with these estimated Stage I parameters, and if we average our observations over census tracts, we obtain a Stage II equation which is easily estimated from census tract statistics:

Eq. 3
$$\left(\overline{R}_t - \sum_j \hat{\alpha}_j \overline{X}_{jt}\right) = \sum_k \beta_k N_{kt} + \overline{f}_t$$

where bars indicate tract averages and where:

$$f_{it} = \epsilon_{it} + \sum_j \left(\alpha_j - \hat{\alpha}_j\right) X_{jit}$$

Since the census tracts contain a varying number of dwelling units (n_t), averaging produces heteroskedasticity; if $E(f^2_{it}) = s^2$, $E(\overline{f}_t^2) = s^2/n_t$. Thus to increase the efficiency of our Stage II estimates, each observation in Equation 3 is weighted by $\sqrt{n_t}$.

Unfortunately, the stepwise regressions described above will normally yield biased estimates of the underlying neighborhood and structural parameters. Using matrix notation, we find that:[8]

and
$$E(\hat{a}) = a + (X'X)^{-1} X'Nb$$
$$E(\hat{b}) = [I - (N'N)^{-1} N'X(X'X)^{-1}X'N]b$$

where "a" and "b" are the set of estimated Stage I and Stage II coefficients.

---

[8] Arthur S. Goldberger, *Econometric Theory* (New York: John Wiley and Sons, Inc., 1964), pp. 194-95.

Unless the neighborhood and the structural attributes are statistically independent (so that X'N = 0) or the matrix of neighborhood parameters is zero (so that b = 0), the estimated coefficients from both regressions will be biased.

The bias in the Stage I parameters reflects the correlation between the structural and the neighborhood attributes of the dwelling unit. For each element in "$\hat{a}$",

$$E(\alpha_j) = \hat{\alpha}_j + \sum_j p_{ij} \beta_j$$

where "p_{ij}" is the coefficient of the "ith" structural variable when the "jth" omitted neighborhood variable is regressed on $\{X\}$.[9] The resulting error in "$R - X\hat{a}$" will bias the Stage II parameters, since part of the contribution of $\{N\}$ is inadvertently captured by the estimated tract residual. The precise nature of this Stage II bias is clearest when "b" is a scalar. In such instances,

$$E(\hat{\beta}) = (1-R_{21}^2) \cdot \beta$$

where "R_{21}^2" is the coefficient of determination from the regression of "N" on "$\{X\}$".[10] Since $0 \leq R_{21}^2 \leq 1$, $\hat{\beta}$ is biased towards zero. Thus, in general, the second stage regression will underestimate the influence of the various neighborhood attributes. The more $\{X\}$ proxies $\{N\}$, the more biased the coefficients.

To control for this bias, neighborhood proxies were added to the Stage I equations. In the 1960 sample, two such variables were used: one signified a white household head; the other, a central city location.

---

[9] Potluri Rao and Roger LeRoy Miller, *Applied Econometrics* (Belmont, California: Wadsworth Publishing Co., 1971), p. 31.

[10] Arthur S. Goldberger, op cit, p. 195.

Although these proxies are admittedly crude, they will hopefully capture most of the correlation between $\{N\}$ and $\{X\}$, thereby reducing (if not eliminating) biases in the estimated State II parameters. In the 1970 equations, these two proxies are replaced by eleven variables that describe many relevant aspects of the dwelling unit's neighborhood. Although certain key omissions necessitate the retention of our two-staged approach, the large number of neighborhood variables included in the 1970 Stage I equations virtually eliminates the possibility of bias in the structural coefficients, which guarantees, in turn, unbiased estimates of the Stage II parameters.[11]

IV. The 1970 Regressions

This section presents tenure-specific Stage I and Stage II equations estimated from data describing rents and housing values in the 1970 Boston metropolitan area. Since this study focuses on the neighborhood attributes of the dwelling unit, the bulk of our discussion is directed towards the Stage II regressions. However, we begin our analysis with a brief review of the 1970 Stage I equations; although the coefficients estimated in these regressions are peripheral to our basic interests, their reliability is crucial, since biases in "α" will bias our estimates of "β".

The remainder of the section provides a detailed analysis of the estimated neighborhood parameters. It begins with a discussion of each of the twelve variables appearing in the Stage II equations, and relates their estimated coefficients to the economic rationale underlying their inclusion in our analysis; it then explores tenure-related differences in the various

---

[11] The precise effect of adding proxies to the Stage I equation is explored in Appendix III.

neighborhood parameters; and, finally, it assesses the overall effect of neighborhood quality on the intra-metropolitan variation of housing prices. At this stage, the discussion of the various ethnic and racial coefficients is somewhat abbreviated. A more detailed interpretation of these differentials is presented in the following section of this paper, where the coefficients obtained in the 1960 and 1970 regressions are compared and related to the growth and the composition of the various groups in question.

A. The 1970 Stage I Regressions

In the first stage of the analysis, we regress rents and housing values on the structural attributes of the dwelling unit, using micro-data obtained from the One-in-a-Hundred Public Use Sample for the Boston Urbanized Area.[12] If the parameter bias is small, the structural coefficients obtained in these regressions provide one with a location-free index of the quality of housing services.

1. The Independent Variables

The twenty-seven independent variables appearing in the 1970 Stage I equations fall into three basic categories. The first set of variables--the structural attributes--describe the physical characteristics of the dwelling unit. Although the twelve variables included in this group provide

---

[12] Normally, File "C" of the 1970 One-in-a-Hundred Public Use Sample does not identify the SMSA of the household. However, the Boston metropolitan area represents an exception to this rule, since units located within its bounds are inadvertently identified by other data contained in the sample. The neighborhood characteristics sample reveals three aspects of the dwelling unit's location: its geographic region (nine classifications); whether or not it is located in an urbanized area; and, if so, the size of the urbanized area in which it is located (three classifications). The New England region contains only one urbanized area with a population of one million or more; all observations falling into this category are located in the Boston urbanized area.

one with a rather detailed description of the housing bundle, they are somewhat incomplete in that they ignore the size, the lot size, and the overall quality of the unit.[13] Hopefully, the influence of these excluded attributes will be captured by variables measuring the number of rooms and baths, and the presence of central heat and air conditioning. As long as the included and excluded structural attributes are highly correlated, such omissions will not bias the Stage II estimates of the neighborhood parameters.

The second set of variables appearing in these regressions attempts to correct for inconsistencies that occur when apparently identical units rent or are valued at different amounts. Two variables are used: one which measures the household's length of residency and one which measures the degree of crowding in the dwelling unit. Note that the rationale for the inclusion of these factors varies somewhat by tenure, as does their expected relationship to the unit's market price.

> Length of Residency: For renters, one would normally expect an inverse relationship between rent and the tenant's length of residency. Long leases often prevent landlords from raising rents to the market level. Even when leases are renewed, landlords are generally reluctant to increase the rent of tenants who have lived in their units for a relatively long period of time. In part, this may reflect lower operating costs, since landlords may be forced to refurbish their apartments less frequently if their turnover is low. The relationship between the household's length of residency and the value of owner-occupied homes is less obvious. Conceivably, this variable may capture systematic errors in the estimated value of the dwelling unit. Past studies have shown that the housing values reported in the

---

[13] For a detailed study of the components of housing quality, see John F. Kain and John M. Quigley, "Measuring the Value of Housing Quality," *Journal of the American Statistical Association*, Vol. 65 (June, 1970), pp. 532-48.

Census often conflict with those estimated by professional assessors.[14] Presumably, values assigned to units purchased within a year or two of the Census will be reasonably accurate. However, if households have occupied their units for a considerable period of time, their estimates may be subject to error. In theory, there is no reason to expect this reporting error to be either positive or negative, so that it is difficult to predict the relationship between length of residency and housing values that might be observed in any sample.

Crowding: If landlords are reluctant to accept households that contribute more than the normal amount of wear-and-tear to their units, rents may rise with the number of persons per room. Unusually heavy use results in higher maintenance expenditures and/or a more rapid depreciation of the unit. Conceivably, part--if not all--of this cost may be borne by the tenant. In the owner's market, the number of persons per room should not affect the value of the unit, since the household views the higher maintenance expenditures associated with crowding as one of his operating costs. However, if over-crowded units tend to be under-maintained and as a result depreciate more rapidly than other units of the same vintage, the crowding variable may proxy some of the omitted quality characteristics of the unit.

The remaining eleven variables describe various aspects of the dwelling unit's environment, and are included in these regressions in order to minimize any biases that might otherwise result from the two-tiered estimating procedure employed by this study. Since these variables are undoubtedly correlated with neighborhood attributes that are excluded from these equations--namely, the cost and the quality of publicly provided goods and services and the ethnic composition of the neighborhood--their estimated coefficients may be subject to considerable bias. Accordingly, the Stage II equations yield more reliable estimates of the variables' true contribution to the price of a dwelling unit.

Neighborhood attributes are included at this stage of our analysis simply to improve our estimates of the structural parameters. Since their

---

[14] Leslie Kish and John B. Lansing, "Response Errors in Estimating the Values of Homes," _Journal of the American Statistical Association_, XLIX (September 1954) pp. 520-38.

coefficients are biased, they are not used to calculate the residuals which form the dependent variable in Stage II. In the calculation of these residuals, the Stage I neighborhood variables are simply set equal to their SMSA mean value for every census tract.

2. The Estimated Parameters

Table 1 presents the 1970 Stage I regression equations for both owner-occupied and rental units. In both regressions, the dependent variable is expressed in logarithmic terms, so that the estimated Stage I (and Stage II) parameters represent the percentage change in price associated with the presence of the various housing attributes. The data used to estimate these equations was obtained from the 1970 One-in-a-Hundred Public Use Sample. In selecting the sample, we omitted group quarters, rental units reporting gross rents under $30, units with no cash rents exclusive of utilities, and units located outside of the Boston Urbanized Area. The final sample contained 3,364 owner-occupied units and 3,985 rental units. Since the 1970 Census does not report the value of owner-occupied units in multi-family structures, the owner equation pertains only to single family units.

Most of the variables appearing in the two equations have the expected sign and are highly significant. Combined, they account for approximately 48% of the variation in gross rents and 57% of the variation in reported housing values. With one or two exceptions, the interpretation of the structural and household variables is relatively straightforward. The unusually large coefficients associated with an extra bathroom, central air conditioning, and complete plumbing facilities probably reflect quality differences not explicitly incorporated into the equations. Bias induced by omitted variables may also explain the rather peculiar age coefficients that were obtained in the renter's equation, where older units appear to

TABLE 1

The 1970 Stage I Regressions

Dependent Variables	Ln(Value)[a]	Ln(Rent)[b]
I. Structural Variables		
Ln(Rooms)[c]	.3625 (16.20)	.3003 (23.49)
Central Heat[d] (Yes = 1)	.0729 (2.173)	.0861 (5.715)
Units in Structure		
a. Duplex (Yes = 1)	---	-.0882 (3.840)
b. Three or more (Yes = 1)	---	-.1119 (4.969)
Central Air Conditioning (Yes = 1)	.1014 (2.240)	.3209 (9.427)
Basement (Yes = 1)	.0919 (3.907)	.0639 (3.151)
Number of Bathrooms		
a. One-and-one-half (Yes = 1)	.1618 (12.38)	.1371 (4.697)
b. Two or more (Yes = 1)	.3196 (19.40)	.2505 (7.394)
Age of Structure		
a. Built 1960-1970 (Yes = 1)	.2097 (12.44)	.1791 (10.52)
b. Built 1950-1959 (Yes = 1)	.1716 (11.63)	-.1332 (6.773)
c. Built 1940-1949 (Yes = 1)	.1132 (6.148)	-.0625 (3.420)
Complete Plumbing Facilities[e] (Yes = 1)	.1799 (2.939)	.2529 (10.58)

TABLE 1 (cont)

II. Household Variables

Crowding

a. Less than 0.5 Persons per Room (Yes = 1)	.0111 (0.318)	-.0593 (6.155)
b. Over 1.0 Persons per Room (Yes = 1)	-.0743 (2.866)	---

Length of Residency

a. Moved in 1950-1964 (Yes = 1)	-.0710 (5.517)	-.1383 (12.05)
b. Moved in Before 1950 (Yes = 1)	-.1120 (6.669)	-.1803 (9.917)

III. Neighborhood Variables

Accessibility Proxies

a. Central City Location (Yes = 1)	-.1258 (6.005)	.0451 (3.766)
b. Proportion of Units in Single-Family Structure	-.0760 (2.332)	-.1225 (3.903)
c. Proportion of Unit in Structures with Five or More Units	.0115 (0.180)	.0966 (3.086)

Demographic Variables

a. Average Neighborhood Income ($1000's)	.0073 (1.828)	.0057 (1.540)
b. Proportion High Status[f]	.0709 (0.597)	.1872 (2.524)
c. Proportion Black	-.0376 (2.013)	-.0799 (1.909)
d. Black Household Head (Yes = 1)	-.0376 (0.540)	.0170 (0.637)
e. Proportion Puerto Rican	-.9848 (2.152)	-.0869 (0.370)

f. Puerto Rican Household Head (Yes = 1)	.0767 (0.665)	.0055 (0.093)
Proportion High-Valued Units[g]	.5422 (8.946)	.5688 (11.65)
Proportion Vacant Units	-2.056 (5.127)	-.7837 (3.903)
Constant	8.670 (102.9)	3.961 (87.16)
F	179.87	140.80
R^2	.57	.48
No. of Observations	3,364	3,985

t-statistics presented in parentheses

[a] The Census lists the reported values in intervals which range from "$0-$5000" to "$50,000 or more". Units were assigned values equal to the midpoint of these intervals in all but two cases. Units falling in the "$0-$5000" range were assigned values of $3,500; units in the "$50,000 or more" range were assigned values of $60,000. This procedure corresponds to that used by the Census when calculating the average values of housing units.

[b] "Rent" refers to gross monthly rent, which is equal to the unit's contract rent plus the value of all utilities purchased by the tenant. In 1970, gross rent data is continuous.

[c] A value of "12" was assigned to units classified as having "nine or more rooms".

[d] Includes steam or hot water, a central warm air furnace, or a built-in electric unit.

[e] Includes each of the following facilities: piped hot and cold water inside the structure; a flush toilet; and a bathtub or shower inside the structure which is used only by the occupants or that structure.

[f] This is a composite variable measuring the occupation and education of households residing in the unit's neighborhood:

$$X = 0.5 (O + E)$$

where O = proportion of workers who are professional, technical, and kindred workers, and managers and administrators except farm; and E = proportion of persons 25-54 years old with four or more years of college.

[g] This variable is a weighted average of the proportion of units with above average values and gross rents:

$$X = p_o(HV) + p_r(HR)$$

where "HV" is the proportion of owner-occupied units with values of $25,000 or more; "HR" is the proportion of renter-occupied units with gross rents of $150 or more; and p_o and p_r are the proportion of the neighborhood's dwelling units that are owner-occupied and rental, respectively.

rent at considerable premiums compared to units constructed in either the forties or fifties. Since one generally expects age to proxy quality, this result seems somewhat surprising. Apparently, the condition of the unit is fairly independent of its age, so that the estimated parameters probably reflect a host of locational and architectural attributes that are correlated with the unit's year of construction.[15]

B. The 1970 Stage II Regressions

In the second stage of our analysis, the structural and household parameters that were estimated in the Stage I regressions are used to calculate an average rent (or value) for each census tract in the Boston SMSA, based on the physical characteristics of the rental (or owner-occupied) units contained in that tract. Our Stage II dependent variable is the difference between the actual and this predicted (logarithm of) rent and in effect, is the tract's rental premium or discount after adjustment for the physical attributes of its dwellings.[16]

The Stage II equations are obtained by regressing these calcualted rent and value residuals on the neighborhood attributes of the tract. Since we retain the semi-log form, the resulting coefficients describe the percentage effect of the various dimensions of neighborhood quality on the market price of the dwelling.

Most of the independent variables appearing in the Stage II equations fall into one of four major categories that reflect (1) the tract's acces-

---

[15] In the owner's market, housing values decline steadily with the dwelling unit's age, reflecting the shorter life expectancies and the higher operating expenditures associated with aging.

[16] Calculation of the dependent variable is described in Appendix IV.

sibility to employment centers; (2) its general physical attractiveness; (3) the demographic characteristics of its residents; and (4) the quality and cost of its publicly provided goods and services. Two additional variables were included in the equations to reflect factors other than neighborhood quality: the vacancy rate and the proportion of all units classified as public housing.

1. The Estimated Parameters

Table 2 presents the Stage II regression results for both owner-occupied and rental units, estimated from data obtained primarily from the 1970 Fourth Count Summary Tapes of the Census of Population and Housing.[17] Each observation corresponds to a census tract in the Boston SMSA. Since the Census occasionally suppressed relevant information on either the housing stock or the population of a given tract, the original sample of 531 tracts was reduced to 480 tracts for owner-occupied units and 501 tracts for rental units. To eliminate the heteroskedascity induced by using average data, the owner and the renter equations are weighted by the square root of the tract's number of owner-occupied and rental units, respectively.[18]

On the whole, these two equations perform rather well, explaining about 70% of the variation in gross rents and housing values that cannot be attributed to differences in the structural characteristics of the tract's dwelling units. In the owners' equation, the variables measuring the tract's

---

[17]Additional data sources included: Gregory K. Ingram, <u>Simulating the Urban Air Pollution Environment</u>, for NSF Grant NSF-GI-29965, "The Automobile and the Regulation of its Impact on the Environment," (August, 1973); The Commonwealth of Massachusetts, Department of Education, <u>Expenditures per Pupil in Average Membership: School Year 1969-1970</u>; Massachusetts Federation of Taxpayers Association, <u>Tax Talk</u>, 1970.

[18]The unweighted regressions are presented in Appendix I.

TABLE 2

The 1970 Stage Two Regressions

Sample	Owners[a]	Renters[b]
Ln (Distance)[c]	-.0977 (4.538)	-.0884 (5.356)
Tax Rate[d] (per $1000 assessed valuation)	-.0017 (3.898)	.0012 (3.769)
Per Pupil Elementary School Expenditures ($100's)	.0320 (6.606)	.0222 (6.140)
Average Income ($1000's)	.0134 (5.835)	.0085 (4.645)
Proportion Low Status[e]	-1.772 (8.667)	-1.521 (12.20)
Proportion Black	-.0807 (1.250)	-.0765 (2.260)
Proportion Other Non-White	2.114 (4.100)	.2693 (1.617)
Proportion Italian[f]	.5119 (4.553)	.0807 (1.227)
Proportion Puerto Rican[f]	-.3692 (1.002)	.3228 (1.661)
Proportion Public Housing	-.0061 (.0571)	-.3207 (6.093)
Proportion Vacant	-1.874 (4.487)	-.1201 (.5250)
Air Pollution[g]	-2.024 (2.289)	-2.011 (3.352)
Constant	.0679 (0.779)	.0672 (1.027)
R^2	.73	.68
F	105.99	81.66
No. of Observations	480	501

TABLE 2 (cont)

[a] Observations weighted by the square root of the number of owner-occupied units in the tract.

[b] Observations weighted by the square root of the number of occupied rental units (with cash rent) in the tract.

[c] "Distance" is a weighted variable defined as:

$$\ln(\text{Distance}_t) = \ln(a_1 x_{1t} + a_2 x_{2t} = \ldots + a_5 x_{5t})$$

where "x_{it}" is the straight-line distance between the tract and the "i^{th}" employment center, and "a_i" is the proportion of total SMSA manufacturing, wholesale, retail, and service employment contained in that center. Five employment centers were selected: Boston, Cambridge, Lynn, Quincy, and Waltham.

[d] The tax rate is the equalized (or full valued) rate, obtained by multiplying the nominal rate by the municipality's average assessment-sales ratio.

[e] The tract's socio-economic status was measured by the following variable:

$$s = .5 \times (E + L)$$

where "E" is the proportion of the tract's residents over twenty-five years of age who have not attended high school, and "L" is the proportion of male workers over fourteen years of age who are classified as laborers.

[f] "Italian" ("Puerto Rican") refers to individuals who were born in Italy (Puerto Rico) or whose parents were born in Italy (Puerto Rico).

[g] The air pollution variable measures the concentration of particulates, measured in milligrams per cubic meter.

concentration of public housing units and Puerto Rican households proved insignificant (at a 30% confidence interval); in the renters' equation, only the vacancy rate failed to exert a noticeable effect on rents. The parameters associated with the remaining variables have the expected signs in each regression and in most instances are highly significant.

a. The Racial and Ethnic Variables

Ethnic and racial premiums appear in both housing submarkets, and are for the most part large and highly significant.[19] According to our estimates, rents and housing values fall with the neighborhood's concentration of blacks and rise with its concentration of Italians, Puerto Ricans, and "Other Non-Whites". This latter group consists mainly of Chinese, and our results are essentially the same if we replace the racial variable with a variable that measures the proportion of the tract's residents who are first and second generation Chinese Americans. Table 3 compares the estimated rent and value differentials that prevail in neighborhoods containing the heaviest concentrations of the various racial and ethnic groups. As the chart readily illustrates, price differentials associated with the ethnic composition of the neighborhood are as large, if not larger than those

---

[19] For each ethnic and racial variable "X", a number of regressions were estimated which used both "X" and "X^2" as explanatory variables, thereby allowing for the u-shaped patterns of rent differentials that might result from preferences for diversity or homogeneity. When the coefficients of "X" and "X^2" had opposite signs, the point of maximum or minimum rents was found by dividing the coefficient of "X" by twice the coefficient of "X^2". If this point lay between zero and the maximum value of "X" observed in the sample, the quadratic form was retained; however in the 1970 sample, this never occurred.

which arise from its concentration of blacks.[20] Indeed, in both housing submarkets, the largest differentials occur in Chinatown, where housing prices are 15% higher for renters and 65% higher for owners than prices in otherwise identical all-white tracts.

TABLE 3

The 1970 Racial and Ethnic Price Differentials

	OWNERS		RENTERS	
	MAXIMUM SAMPLE CONCENTRATION	MAXIMUM PREMIUM(+) OR DISCOUNT(-)	MAXIMUM SAMPLE CONCENTRATION	MAXIMUM PREMIUM(+) OR DISCOUNT(-)
Blacks	1.00	-8%	1.00	-8%
Italians	.55	+28%	.69	+6%
Puerto Rican	--	--	.36	+11%
Chinese	.31	+65%	.57	+15%

Unfortunately, these racial and ethnic price differentials prove difficult to decipher. On the surface, they appear to reflect market externalities, where whites avoid contact with blacks and where Puerto Ricans, Italians, and Chinese prefer their established ethnic neighborhoods to the diversity of the greater society. However, although such hypotheses are reasonable, they can not be supported on a statistical basis alone since some, if not all, of the observed premiums may reflect factors other than externalities.

---

[20] These differences may have a very simple explanation. In the short run, premiums will reflect supply as well as demand. Thus, the relatively small differentials that were associated with predominantly white neighborhoods may simply reflect the fact that the supply of housing in these areas is relatively elastic compared to the supply of housing in the dense, centrally located Italian and Chinese tracts. However, since differences in demand could also account for the observed parameters differences, this conclusion is somewhat speculative.

The aggregated data employed in our Stage II regressions does not distinguish between premiums that are attached to the neighborhood and premiums that are attached to the household.[21] The latter--known as "discriminatory markups"--reflect systematic differences in the price that households pay for a particular dwelling unit, and presumably arise from the discriminatory behavior of landlords and housing sellers. Since aggregation will obscure the distinction between these two kinds of premiums, in any given neighborhood average rents may be high because a large fraction of its inhabitants are victims of discrimination or because the area itself commands a substantial premium.

According to our Stage I regressions, neither Puerto Ricans nor blacks pay markups of this sort.[22] Since compared to the Italians and the Chinese, these two groups seem particularly susceptible to market discrimination, the ethnic and racial differentials that were observed in the second stage of the analysis are probably neighborhood premiums.

Yet even if we ignore the possible effects of discriminatory markups, analysis remains difficult. In long run equilibrium, demographic price differentials will necessarily reflect household preferences, but in the short run the effects of externalities may be modified by temporary or chronic disturbances in the market. If these disturbances are large enough or persistent enough, rent differentials may arise that are inconsistent with household tastes. Over time, the market will act to eliminate these

---

[21] For two of the few statistical attempts to distinguish the two effects, Martin J. Bailey, "Note on the Economics of Residential Zoning and Urban Renewal," *Land Economics*, Vol. XXXV (August, 1969), pp. 288-92; and Thomas King and Peter Mieszkowski, "Racial Discrimination, Segregation, and the Price of Housing," *Journal of Political Economy*, 81, May/June 1973.

[22] In both the owner and the renter equations, dummies signifying a black and a Puerto Rican household head were insignificant.

temporary differentials, as households change their zone of residence and as the stock of housing expands in areas of excess demand. However, when the mobility of households is limited and when the supply of housing is inelastic, this adjustment process may be painfully slow.

Racial and ethnic minorities seem particularly vulnerable to this kind of disturbance. The mobility of recent immigrants may be restricted by inadequate knowledge of the housing opportunities available throughout the city; the mobility of other groups--most notably blacks--by the discriminatory practices of realtors, landlords, and financial institutions. In such instances, if the supply of housing in minority neighborhoods is relatively inelastic and if the inflow of migrants is large relative to the existing number of dwellings, short run differentials can arise in the absence of externalities.[23] Since restricted mobility will also foster racial and ethnic segregation, the effects of these two phenomena are often indistinguishable.

Accordingly, the racial and ethnic premiums which were observed in our two samples may simply reflect an excess demand for housing in tracts whose residents are unusually immobile. While this argument does not pertain to the differentials that are associated with the predominantly white neighborhoods, it may relate to the other ethnic and racial premiums. In the following section of the paper, we will explore this possibility by relating changes in the estimated differentials to the composition and growth of the various ethnic groups. At this point, suffice it to say that demographic factors play a significant role in the determination of housing rents and

---

[23] See Gary Becker, <u>The Economics of Discrimination</u> (Chicago: University of Chicago Press, 1957), pp. 78-89; Robert A. Haugen and A. Jones Heins, "A Market Separation Theory of Rent Differentials in Metropolitan Areas," <u>The Quarterly Journal of Economics</u>, Vol. LXXVIII (November, 1964), pp. 660-72.

values.

b. Socio-Economic Status

Ceteris paribus, units located in census tracts with higher family incomes have higher market rents and values. In the Boston SMSA, average tract incomes ranged from a low of $5,271 to a high of $39,384. According to our estimates, this differential alone could account for a 44% difference in housing values and a 29% difference in rents. Of course, part of this differential undoubtedly reflects amenity variables excluded from the equation, in addition to any inherent desire of households to live in high status neighborhoods. Because of the many dimensions of neighborhood quality which elude statistical quantification, it seems doubtful that regression analysis can ever isolate the pure neighborhood effect of average tract income.

The status variable may more accurately reflect the household's desire to live in prestigious neighborhoods. Given the income of the tract, the larger the proportion of low status households, the lower its average rent. In the Boston SMSA, the variable ranged from 2 to 39 percent, inducing rent and value differentials of some 56 percent. Thus, according to our estimates, social status exerts an independent influence on the location decisions of households. However, one should note that its coefficient may also be subject to considerable bias. High status households with low current incomes most likely have high permanent incomes. To the extent that permanent income is correlated with the omitted neighborhood amenities, the coefficient of the status term will be biased and will overstate the depressing effect of concentrations of low status households.

c. Accessibility

Ceteris paribus, housing values and rent increase with the tract's accessibility to employment centers. According to our estimates, dwelling units situated in the most accessible tract sell for about 21% more and rent for about 23% more than otherwise identical units located in the tract farthest from concentrations of employment.[24] These observed premiums are consistent with traditional models of urban spatial structure, which contend that households bid up the price of accessible locations in their effort to minimize the time and the out-of-pocket costs of commuting to work.[25]

    d. The Fiscal Variables

At first glance, the coefficients of the tax and expenditure variables seem highly plausible and appear to confirm a number of hypotheses concerning the location decisions of households and the provision of locally provided goods and services. According to an argument originally formulated by Charles Tiebout, units located in municipalities offering unusually attractive fiscal packages will rent or sell at a premium.[26] Thus, for a given tax rate, prices should rise with the quality of public output; and, for a given level of that output, fall with increases in the associated cost to the household. Since property taxes are levied on the landlord rather than the tenant, the implied relationship between housing prices and inter-community tax differentials will vary by tenure. In the owner's market, one expects an inverse correlation between the two variables, since higher

---

[24] In the 1960 sample, the coefficient of this variable was significant, but positive. Since the variables included in the two sets of regressions are essentially the same, this result is puzzling, and makes the 1970 coefficients less convincing.

[25] William Alonso, <u>Location and Land Use</u> (Cambridge: Harvard University Press, 1964). Edwin Mill, "An Aggregative Model of Resource Allocation in a Metropolitan Area," <u>American Economic Review</u>, Vol. LVII, (May 1967), pp. 197-211. Richard Muth, <u>Cities and Housing</u> (Chicago: University of Chicago Press, 1969).

[26] Charles Tiebout, "A Pure Theory of Local Expenditures," <u>Journal of Political Economy</u>, Vol. 64 (Octover, 1956), pp. 416-24.

taxes will probably be capitalized into lower housing values. In the rental market, the nature of this relationship depends on the landlord's ability to pass on his tax, which reflects the elasticities of the demand and supply of rental housing services within a given community.[27] Assuming a relatively elastic demand and a relatively inelastic supply, tenants will pay a small, but significant fraction of the existing tax differentials.

Although our tax and expenditure variables behave according to this theory, their coefficients may be somewhat unreliable, and may reflect factors other than the simple capitalization of the community's fiscal attractiveness. The simultaneous determination of the tax rate, the value of dwelling units, and the level of public spending makes the single equation model inappropriate, in that it implies a correlation between the equation's error term and the tax and expenditure variables that may bias the estimated fiscal coefficients.[28] Numerous techniques exist which would produce consistent (though still biased) estimates of the true parameters. However, the implementation of any of these procedures requires the construction of an auxiliary set of equations explaining the determination of a community's tax and expenditure mix. Since past studies have shown that a somewhat simplified application of this more sophisticated technique does little to alter the estimated coefficients and since the fiscal variables are somewhat peripheral to our primary interests, we retained the single

---

[27] Larry L. Orr, "The Incidence of Differential Property Taxes on Urban Housing," *National Tax Journal*, Vol. XXX (September, 1968), pp. 253-62.

[28] Wallace Oates, "The Effect of Property Taxes and Local Public Spending on Property Values," *Journal of Political Economy*, Vol. LXXVII (November/December, 1969), p. 963.

equation model.[29] According to our equations, only about 10 percent of intercommunity tax differentials are born by rental households, and only about 20 percent of these differentials are capitalized into lower housing values.[30]

e. Air Pollution

Ceteris paribus, increased air pollution reduces rents and housing values. In the Boston SMSA, the concentration of particulates ranged from a low of .042 to a high of .100 milligrams per cubic meter. According to our estimates, units located in the heavily polluted zones would rent or sell for about 11.7 percent less than otherwise identical units located in a relatively pollution-free tract. Part of this differential may reflect externalities associated with the concentration of non-residential activities that no doubt accompanies the perceived decline in air quality, and part may reflect the overall quality of the landscape and the general layout of streets, homes, and open spaces.

---

[29] Two studies have tested the sensitivity of the 1960 Boston data to simultaneity bias: both found that the two-staged procedure did little to alter the estimated tax and expenditures coefficients. See J. D. Heinberg and W. E. Oates, "The Incidence of Differential Property Taxes on Urban Housing: A Comment and Some Further Evidence", National Tax Journal, Vol. XXIII (March 1970) pp. 92-98; Larry L. Orr, "The Incidence of Differential Property Taxes: A Response", National Tax Journal, Vol. XXIII (March 1970) pp. 99-101.

[30] In 1970, the typical owner-occupied dwelling unit in the Boston SMSA had a value of about $23,000. According to our estimates, an increase in the property tax from six to seven percent would decrease the value of such a unit by $391. If the tax were fully capitalized, its value would fall by approximately $1,840, assuming a life expectancy of forty years and a five percent discount rate. (Wallace Oates, op. cit., p. 965.) Similarly, in 1970, the average unit rented for about $140 per month. Assuming a rent-value ratio of .0075 (the calculated sample average), such a unit would be worth $18,667, so that a $10 tax increase would raise annual rents by $20.16 and annual taxes by $186.67.

f. Vacancy Rate

According to our estimates, owner-occupied units located in the tract with the highest vacancy rate (21 percent) will sell for about 40 percent less than otherwise identical units located in tracts where the market is unusually tight. This inverse relationship may reflect a number of factors, including parameter bias. On the one hand, a high vacancy rate may be evidence of a localized excess supply of housing which in the short run depresses rents and values of both occupied and unoccupied units. Alternatively, the vacancy rate may be proxying certain omitted variables--particularly vandalism--that exert a negative influence on housing prices.

g. Public Housing

The variable reflecting the concentration of public housing units proved significant for renters and insignificant for owners. This differential effect may have a rather simple explanation. Presumably, a tract's concentration of public housing can have two effects on its calculated average rent. Since publicly owned units are supposedly priced at below-market rates and since the rent on these units is included in the Census' calculation of the average level of rents prevailing in the tract, areas with large concentration of public housing will automatically have lower average rents. In addition to this direct effect, negative externalities may be attached to public housing *per se*; this secondary effect may produce further reductions in the level of rents prevailing in the tract.

For owner-occupied units, only this latter effect is present. Thus, according to our estimates, the concentration of public housing *per se* does not affect the value of owner-occupied units. Given the socio-economic status of the tract's residents (which of course will be low in areas with public housing), the presence or absence of publicly owned units has no perceivable influence on market housing values. If these external effects are also absent in the rental housing market, the estimated coefficient implies that publicly owned housing units in the Boston SMSA rent for an average of 32 percent less than otherwise identical privately owned units.

2. Differentials in the Estimated Coefficients

As Table 2 readily illustrates, most of the estimated Stage II owner and renter coefficients display a remarkable degree of similarity. Accessibility, per pupil school expenditures, air pollution, and the concentration of blacks and low status households all have approximately the same proportional effect on gross monthly rents and on the value of owner-occupied dwellings. Three additional variables have coefficients with the same sign but with fairly pronounced differences in magnitude; the estimated coefficients of the variables reflecting the tract's income, its concentration of Chinese, and its concentration of Italians all are significantly larger in the owner than in the renter equation. Four remaining variables appear to have markedly different effects on the market price of owner-occupied and rental units. The coefficient of the tax variable is significantly different from zero in each regression, but with the opposite sign; the vacancy variable is significant for owners but insignificant for renters; and, finally, a tract's concentration of Puerto Ricans and public housing units have a noticeable effect on rents but prove insignificant in the equation explaining the value of owner-occupied units.

Most of the observed differences in the two sets of parameters prove difficult to interpret. A priori reasonong can be used to predict differential effects for only two of the twelve variables appearing in the equations--the tax rate and the proportion of units in the tract that are publicly owned. Any differences in the remaining coefficients reflect a multitude of factors that are normally indistinguishable. The estimated parameters depend upon the underlying demand and supply conditions in the two housing submarkets;

differences in these markets should induce differences in the coefficients appearing in the two equations. Unless one is willing to make some rather restrictive assumptions about the similarities of the owner and renter markets, the hedonic price index is under-identified and the observed differentials cannot be attributed to specific differences in either the demand for or the supply of the two types of housing.[31]

3. The Dependent Variables

The overall effect of the neighborhood variables on the intrametropolitan variation in housing prices can be illustrated by a comparison of the prices that are predicted from the structural attributes alone ($\hat{R}_s = \Sigma \hat{\alpha} \bar{X}$) and from the full set of attributes ($\hat{R}_F = \Sigma \hat{\alpha} \bar{X} + \Sigma \hat{\beta} N$). In each housing submarket, the standard deviation of "$\hat{R}_s$" ($13.86 for renters; $3,166 for owners) is significantly less than the standard deviation of "$\hat{R}_F$" ($27.34 for renters; $8,254 for owners), so that apparently, neighborhood effects increase the variance of housing values and rents. Were prices based solely on the structural attributes of the unit, they would cluster more tightly around their average SMSA values.

One might also ask whether or not, on a tract level, "large" structural bundles tend to be found in high quality neighborhoods. The structure of this study lends itself well to this sort of analysis, since predicted tract

---

[31] For example, if renters and owners have approximately the same attitudes towards the ethnic mix of their neighborhoods, the larger premium associated with Italian tracts that appears in the owner equation may simply reflect a relative scarcity of owner-occupied units in these centrally located, relative high-density areas. On the other hand, if one assumes that both markets are in long-run equilibrium, one may attribute the observed differential to systematic differences in either the tastes or the incomes of households in the two housing markets. Although the first explanation is intuitively more appealing, one cannot dismiss the possibility of systematic differences in the underlying demand curves of the two groups.

rents ($\hat{R}_s = \Sigma \hat{\alpha} \bar{X}$) and the calculated tract residuals ($D = \bar{R} - \hat{R}_s$) serve as convenient indices to the size of the housing bundle and to the overall quality of its environment. In the 1970 sample, the simple correlation coefficient of these two composite variables was 0.63 for owners and 0.37 for renters, indicating a general tendency for large bundles to be located in expensive neighborhoods.

Table 4 provides a more detailed representation of the relationship between bundle size and the various neighborhood attributes. In that chart, tracts are divided into five equi-sized groups according to their predicted rent or value; the columns depict the average values of the various neighborhood attributes for tracts contained in each of these five categories. The general pattern is the same for owners and renters. In both markets, large bundles of housing services tend to be located in areas displaying a multitude of environmental amenities; indeed, it is precisely this tendency which underlies the differential dispersion of "$\hat{R}_s$" and "$\hat{R}_F$".[32]

V. A Comparison of the 1960 and 1970 Stage II Regressions.

In this section, equations similar to those presented above are re-estimated using data obtained primarily from the 1960 Census of Population and

---

[32] Neighborhood effects will almost always increase the variance in rents. Suppose $R_i = aX_i + bN_i$, where $a, b > 0$. Then:

$$VAR(R) = a^2 VAR(X) + b^2 VAR(N) + 2ab\, COV(X,N)$$

If rents were based on the structural attributes alone, $VAR(R) = a^2 VAR(X)$. If rents depend on the full set of attributes, the variance will increase unless 1) $COV(X,N) < 0$ and 2) $b^2 VAR(N) < 2a \cdot |COV(X,N)|$. Thus, the stronger the correlation between "X" and "N", the larger the variance in rents.

Table 4

DISTRIBUTION OF NEIGHBORHOOD ATTRIBUTES BY BUNDLE SIZE
IN THE 1970 SAMPLE[a]

	I (SMALL)	II	III (AVERAGE)	IV	V (LARGE)
Distance to CBD (Miles)	3.6 (3.1)	5.8 (5.8)	7.3 (7.2)	9.0 (9.9)	11.9 (12.0)
Tax Rate (per $1000 Assed Valuation)	85.07 (84.16)	70.02 (73.19)	67.90 (69.57)	60.08 (56.38)	50.37 (47.66)
Per Pupil Elementary School Expenditures	847.80 (873.31)	826.04 (818.98)	787.03 (767.69)	807.43 (769.64)	862.37 (911.62)
Average Income	10,065 (9,039)	11,103 (10,139)	11,659 (11,210)	13,296 (13,085)	16,652 (18,649)
% Low Status	20.4 (22.3)	15.1 (17.2)	14.0 (12.8)	10.6 (10.1)	7.4 (5.7)
% Black	8.9 (6.5)	4.6 (8.6)	8.6 (8.1)	6.7 (4.1)	3.0 (0.7)
% Italian	12.3 (11.8)	7.7 (8.0)	7.7 (7.2)	6.4 (6.5)	5.1 (3.9)
% Puerto Rican	2.6 (3.6)	2.0 (1.9)	1.5 (1.3)	1.0 (0.8)	1.0 (0.8)
% Other Non-White	2.5 (1.7)	0.7 (0.6)	0.4 (0.6)	0.7 (0.5)	0.5 (0.7)
% Public Housing	6.1 (3.2)	2.2 (2.6)	1.4 (2.4)	0.5 (0.6)	0.2 (0.1)
% Vacant	5.7 (4.5)	2.9 (3.0)	2.3 (2.8)	1.9 (1.8)	1.2 (1.1)
Air Pollution	.078 (.085)	.070 (.070)	.065 (.065)	.060 (.057)	.052 (.053)
Residual	−.086 (−.408)	−.053 (−.225)	−.037 (−.104)	+.031 (−.012)	+.107 (.181)
% Owner-Occupied	22.1 (24.5)	40.5 (35.7)	49.6 (49.5)	60.1 (66.2)	75.5 (75.9)

[a] Bracketed figures pertain to owner-occupied units; unbracketed figures pertain to rental units.

Housing. Theoretically, a comparison of the 1960 and 1970 Stage II regression coefficients can lend considerable insight into the interpretation of the racial and ethnic premiums that were observed in the 1970 sample. The previous discussion emphasized the difficulties involved in distinguishing between price differentials which reflect externalities in the housing market and differentials which merely arise from a temporary (or perhaps chronic) market disequilibrium. Knowledge of the change--if any--in the size of the demographic coefficients, coupled with a history of the growth and the composition of the various ethnic and racial groups, can conceivably facilitate the interpretation of the observed market discounts and premiums.

Unfortunately, the 1960 Census data contains a number of deficiencies which necessitate the adoption of a somewhat modified estimating procedure. The resulting equations differ from earlier ones in two major respects: neighborhood proxies representing a white household head and a central city location replace the eleven neighborhood variables previously appearing in the Stage I regressions;[33] and tenure groups are merged in the Stage II equations. To facilitate our time-series analysis, the 1970 regressions are also re-estimated according to this technique. Since either revision can bias the estimated neighborhood parameters, an examination of the nature and of the extent of these biases seems a prerequisite to any comparison of the estimated Stage II parameters.

A. Parameter Bias in the Revised Stage II Equations

Using the 1970 equations, one can test for some of the biases inherent in our revised estimating procedure. If the two neighborhood proxies to be

---

[33] Since the 1960 Public Use Sample does not identify the SMSA of the household, the 1960 Stage I equations are estimated from a sample drawn from each of the eight metropolitan areas in Massachusetts.

included in the Stage I equations fail to capture the correlation between the structural and the neighborhood attributes of the housing bundle, the two-staged regressions will produce biased estimates of the true parameters. In particular, if part of a neighborhood variable's effect is inadvertently incorporated into the Stage I estimates of the structural parameters, its coefficient in the Stage II equation will be biased towards zero. In the 1970 regressions that were presented earlier in this paper, the possibility of such a bias is virtually eliminated; by including a large number of neighborhood attributes in the Stage I equations, one obtains reasonably unbiased estimates of both the Stage I and Stage II parameters.

Table 5 compares the Stage II neighborhood parameters produced by each of these two techniques. On the whole, the estimated coefficients are remarkably similar; in most instances, any bias that does occur has the expected sign and appears to be rather small. However, in the renters' equation the size and the significance of the estimated coefficient of one variable--the tract's concentration of other non-whites--is substantially reduced when proxies replace the expanded set of neighborhood variables in the Stage I regressions. This phenomenon should emphasize the fact that the coefficients obtained in the 1960 Stage II equation and in its 1970 counterpart represent lower bounds of the true parameters. Although this bias is generally unimportant, in a few instances it can produce misleading results.

Combining tenure groups at the tract level may also bias the estimated parameters, although the precise effects of such a procedure are not immediately clear. The merging technique employed in this analysis is relatively simple: using the estimated Stage I equations, one calculates a rent-value ratio for each census tract in the SMSA, based on the structural characteristics of the dwelling units contained in the tract; given this ratio, one converts

Table 5

A COMPARISON OF THE 1970 STAGE II COEFFICIENTS OBTAINED
WITH DIFFERENT STAGE I NEIGHBORHOOD VARIABLES

	RENTERS		OWNERS	
	PROXIES ONLY	EXPANDED SET	PROXIES ONLY	EXPANDED SET
Ln (Distance)	-.0812 (5.025)	-.0884 (5.0356)	-.1032 (4.811)	-.0766 (4.538)
Tax Rate	.0012 (3.942)	.0012 (3.769)	-.0017 (3.915)	-.0017 (3.893)
Per Pupil Elementary School Expenditures ($100's)	.0212 (5.991)	.0222 (6.140)	.0308 (6.379)	.0320 (6.606)
Average Income ($1000's)	.0071 (3.962)	.0085 (4.645)	.0085 (3.684)	.0134 (5.835)
Proportion Low Status	-1.320 (10.81)	-1.521	-1.603 (7.872)	-1.772 (8.667)
Proportion Black	-.0647 (1.952)	-.0765 (2.260)	-.1042 (1.620)	-.0807 (1.250)
Proportion Other Non-White	.1385 (0.850)	.2693 (1.617)	2.039 (3.970)	2.114 (4.100)
Proportion Italian	.1338 (2.077)	.0807 (1.227)	.0586 (4.541)	.5119 (4.553)
Proportion Puerto Rican	.2830 (1.487)	.3228 (1.661)	-.3959 (1.087)	-.3692 (1.002)
Proportion Public Housing	-.3381 (6.562)	-.3207 (6.093)	-.0423 (0.396)	-.0061 (.0571)
Proportion Vacant	-.3081 (2.773)	-.1201 (3.352)	-2.007 (2.216)	-2.024 (2.890)
Constant	.0420 (0.656)	.0672 (1.027)	.1496 (1.724)	.0679 (.7795)
R^2	.62	.68	.68	.73
F	66.73	81.66	83.55	105.99
No. of Observations	501	501	480	480

market values into market rents, and then combines these imputed rents with the gross rents actually attached to the tract's rental units.[34] In general, it is difficult to predict the precise outcome of this procedure, given that at least one of the Stage II parameters varies by tenure. Since the econometrics involved in merging quickly become unmanageable, no simple formula exists which relates the underlying coefficients of the owner and renter equations to the estimated parameters of the combined regressions. At best, one is left with the rather general notion that the resulting coefficients represent a weighted average of the actual tenure-specific parameters.

Table 6 compares the coefficients derived when separate regressions are run on owners and renters with those obtained when the two groups are combined at the tract level. Two different "combined" regressions are presented in the chart. The first (Type I) shows the full effect of our revised estimating procedure; neighborhood proxies are used in its underlying Stage I regressions and tenure groups are merged at the second stage of the analysis. The second (Type II) is somewhat altered in order to isolate the effect of merging per se; in this regression, the structural parameters which are used to calculate the tract residuals are derived from Stage I equations that include the expanded set of neighborhood variables, thereby minimizing any biases that might otherwise result from the two-tiered estimating procedure. To allow for the differential effect of taxes on housing values and rents, we include a tax (t) and a tax-interaction term ($z = t \cdot \frac{\text{owner-occupied units}}{\text{total units}}$), so that $(\frac{d \text{ Rent}}{\text{Rent}}) / dt = \alpha$ and $(\frac{d \text{ Value}}{\text{Value}}) / dt = \alpha + \beta$ where "α" and "β" are the coefficients of "t" and "z", respectively.

A comparison of the last three columns in Table 6 indicates that merging tenure groups is a fairly harmless simplification. Variables that are

---

[34]Appendix V provides a detailed description of this merging technique.

Table 6

A COMPARISON OF THE COEFFICIENTS OBTAINED IN THE 1970
TENURE-SPECIFIC AND COMBINED REGRESSIONS

	Type I Combined[a]	Type II Combined[a]	Renters[b]	Owners[c]
Ln (Distance)	-.0515 (3.649)	-.0436 (3.042)	-.08884 (5.356)	-.0977 (4.538)
Tax Rate	.0015 (4.574)	.0017 (5.219)	.0012 (3.769)	-.0017 (3.898)
(Tax Rate) (Proportion Owner-Occupied	-.0041[d] (9.463)	-.0046[e] (10.51)	------	------
Per Pupil School Expenditures ($100's)	.0206 (7.025)	.0219 (7.379)	.0222 (6.140)	.0320 (6.606)
Average Income ($1000's)	.0153 (10.40)	.0188 (12.55)	.0085 (4.645)	.0134 (5.835)
Proportion Public Housing	-.2704 (5.274)	-.2420 (4.650)	-.3207 (6.093)	-.0061 (.0571)
Proportion Other Non-White	.2210 (0.904)	.4028 (1.623)	.2693 (1.617)	2.114 (4.100)
Proportion Black	-.0488 (1.471)	-.0348 (1.233)	-.0765 (2.260)	-.0807 91.250)
Proportion Low Status	-1.434 (12.39)	-1.632 (13.90)	-1.521 (12.20)	-1.772 (8.667)
Proportion Italian	.3347 (4.914)	.3391 (4.905)	.0807 (1.227)	.5119 (4.553)
Proportion Puerto Rican	.2006 (1.032)	.2527 (1.281)	.3228 (1.661)	-.3692 (1.002)
Proportion Vacant	-1.017 (4.396)	-.9430 (4.016)	-.1201 (.5250)	-1.874 (4.487)
Air Pollution	-2.116 (4.097)	-2.280 (4.350)	-2.010 (3.352)	-2.024 (2.289)
Constant	.0612 (1.154)	.0068 (0.126)	.0672 (1.027)	.0679 (0.780)

Table 6 (cont'd)

R^2	.79	.83	.68	.73
F	137.85	171.28	81.66	105.99
No. of Observations	478	478	501	480

[a] Weighted by the square root of the number of occupied units in the tract.

[b] Weighted by the square root of the number of occupied rental units in the tract.

[c] Weighted by the square root of the number of owner-occupied units in the tract.

[d] A test that the sum of the coefficients of the tax and the tax interaction terms is equal to zero yields a t-statistic of "-7.37". For owners, the estimated coefficient of the tax variable is "-.0026".

[e] A test that the sum of the coefficients of the tax and the tax interaction terms is equal to zero yields a t-statistic of "-8.52". For owners, the estimated coefficient of the tax variable is "-.0029".

significant in either the owner or the renter equation remain significant when the two submarkets are combined. More important, each of the coefficients in the combined equation has the sign and, in many instances, the approximate magnitude that one might predict from an *a priori* inspection of the tenure-specific parameters. Most of the "combined" parameters are bracketed by the corresponding coefficients from the owner and renter equations; when they lie beyond this range, the discrepancies do not appear to be major. Differences in the parameters yielded by the Type I and the Type II combined regressions reflect additional biases associated with the two-tiered structure of this analysis. A comparison of these two sets of coefficients supports our earlier premise that this bias is generally small.

Thus, the biases inherent in our revised estimating procedure do not seem particularly serious. In the 1970 sample, the coefficients produced by this technique appear to be weighted averages of the underlying tenure-specific parameters; and, although each parameter is subject to a possible downward bias, this bias seems to be rather small. Nevertheless, the procedure's basic validity does not guarantee the direct comparability of parameters estimated from the 1960 and 1970 samples. A direct comparison of these coefficients requires each of the following conditions to hold:

(1) The weights given to owner-occupied and rental units in the "combined" regression must remain the same, so that changes in the "combined" coefficients will always reflect changes in the underlying tenure-specific coefficients.

(2) The correlation between the structural variables, the Stage I neighborhood proxies and the set of neighborhood variables appearing in the Stage II equations must remain the same, so that the bias attached to each of the estimated neighborhood coefficients is identical in both years.

(3) The correlation between the set of neighborhood variables included and excluded from the Stage II regression must remain the same, so that biases produced by omitted Stage II variables remain constant.

Since there is no guarantee that any of these criteria holds, any comparison of the two sets of parameters must necessarily be broad. In general, one can infer very little from small or even moderate changes in the estimated coefficients. These are best viewed as lower bounds to the underlying parameters; changes in their size may sometimes reflect changes in parameter bias, rather than changes in the price structure of the Boston metropolitan area.

B. Differentials in the Estimated Parameters

Table 7 presents the estimated coefficients from the 1960 and the 1970 Stage II regressions.[35] These two regressions are essentially equivalent: two simple neighborhood proxies are included in the Stage I equations, and owners and renters are combined at the tract level. The 1960 equation differs slightly from its more recent counterpart in that the air pollution variable is replaced by two variables measuring the tract's concentration of commercial and manufacturing activity.[36] However, since the land use and the presence of particulate pollution are highly correlated, this substitution should do little to alter the estimated coefficients of the remaining neighborhood attributes.

With two exceptions the estimated relationship between housing prices and the non-demographic variables included in these regressions is approximately the same in the two sample years. Major differences arise only in the

---

[35] The underlying Stage I regressions are presented in Appendix II.

[36] Data was obtained from two sources. For suburban Boston, the <u>1963 Metropolitan District Planning Commission Land Use Survey</u> provided data on land use for each of the seventy-five suburban municipalities. Within a given town, the various census tracts were assumed to have identical land use patterns. For the city of Boston, a compatible 1963 Boston Redevelopment Authority survey was used. This survey divided the city into fourteen approximately homogeneous districts that contained an average of eleven tracts apiece. Separate land use data for available for each of these districts.

Table 7

A COMPARISON OF THE 1960 AND THE 1970 STAGE II REGRESSIONS

	1960	1970
Ln (Distance)	.0223 (2.089)	-.0515 (3.649)
Tax Rate	.0014 (3.980)	.0015 (4.574)
(Tax Rate) · (Proportion Owner-Occupied)	-.0053 (10.54)	-.0041 (9.463)
Per Pupil School Expenditures ($100's)	.0048 (0.755)	.0206 (7.025)
Average Income ($1000's)	.0444 (18.27)	.0153 (10.40)
Proportion Low Status	-.9257 (12.24)	-1.434 (12.39)
Proportion Other Non-White	.6745 (6.710)	.2210 (0.904)
Proportion Black	-.1166 (1.490)	-.0488 (1.471)
(Proportion Black)^2	.2392 (2.280)	---
Proportion Italian	.2032 (5.568)	.3347 (4.914)
Proportion Puerto Rican	.0716 (0.076)	.2006 (1.032)
Proportion Vacant	-.3564 (1.916)	-1.017 (4.396)
Proportion Public Housing	-.3176 (10.08)	-.2704 (5.274)
Proportion Commercial	-.1176 (1.476)	---

Table 7 (cont'd)

Proportion Manufacturing	-.5963 (3.862)	---
Air Pollution	---	-2.116 (4.097)
Constant	-.1176 (2.971)	.0612 (1.154)
R^2	.87	.79
F	194.95	137.9
No. of Observations	436	478

estimated coefficients of the accessibility and the school expenditures variables. In 1960, rents appear to increase with the tract's distance from established centers of employment; in 1970, the opposite is true. Similarly, in 1960, school expenditures seem to exert a negligible influence on average tract rents, while in 1970 their effect is highly significant. These changes most likely reflect changes in parameter bias, rather than changes in the underlying structure of housing values and rents in the Boston metropolitan area. Why this bias has changed in the two sample years is a matter for some speculation.

The racial and ethnic premiums that were observed in the 1970 sample reappear in the 1960 equations, where significant differentials are associated with black, Italian, and Chinese neighborhoods. Theoretically, any comparison of these two parameter sets encounters the same ambiguities of our earlier cross-sectional analysis. Even in the absence of parameter bias, changes in the coefficients may reflect a variety of factors: (1) changes in the attitudes of certain households towards the demographic mix of their neighborhoods; (2) changes in the underlying demand or supply of housing in certain types of neighborhoods; and perhaps (3) changes in discriminatory markups. Nevertheless, in a few instances, if we relate these differentials to the growth and the composition of the various racial and ethnic groups, we can narrow the range of factors that contribute to the observed demographic premiums.

1. Proportion Black

In the 1960 sample, the relationship between housing prices and the proportion black assumed a u-shaped pattern, with minimum rents in neighborhoods that were 25 percent black and with rents in the ghetto some 12 percent higher than rents in otherwise identical all-white zones.[37] In the 1970 sample, these premiums disappeared and prices declined steadily with the tract's concentration of blacks, with ghetto rents at least 5 percent less than rents in the white interior.

The ghetto markups that were observed in the 1960 sample may simply reflect market externalities, where blacks preferred living in segregated neighborhoods, perhaps due to the psychic costs of entering a white or a predominately white neighborhood. However, since the size of those markups would then imply a greater willingness on the part of blacks to pay for racially homogeneous zones, this hypothesis seems somewhat simplistic. Presumably, part of those premiums stemmed from a shortage of housing in tracts with a black majority, rather than or in addition to a tendency on the part of blacks to avoid integration.[38] Although in 1960 predominately black neighborhoods displayed a relatively high overall vacancy rate, their relative abundance of low quality, deteriorating units probably masked an excess demand for units in the average to the above-average quality range.

Accordingly, it seems reasonable to assume that the observed decline in the relative price of ghetto housing arose from decreased pressures within the ghetto, due to a diminished demand for housing by blacks or to a rapid expansion of the stock. Of these two possibilities, only the latter is relevant. Between 1950 and 1960, the number of blacks in the Boston SMSA

---

[38] The possibility that these premiums reflect discriminatory markups can most likely be dismissed. If landlords believe that an influx of blacks will decrease the rental value of their property, they may rent to blacks only at a premium, so that in predominantly white neighborhoods, blacks may fall victim to large discriminatory markups. (Gary Becker, op. cit.) Yet, in established ghetto areas the economic rational for these markups disappears, since an additional black can do little to effect the overall desirability of the landlord's property. This, coupled with the increased bargaining position of black households in predominantly black neighborhoods, makes markups within the ghetto somewhat improbable. If they exist at all, discriminatory premiums are more likely to occur in neighborhoods where the majority of households are white.

grew by some 50 percent (compared to 8.3 percent for whites); and between 1960 and 1970, by some 62 percent (compared to 4.6 percent for whites). Since blacks remained highly concentrated throughout the two decades, rising incomes coupled with this rising growth rate increased rather than decreased the overall demand for housing within established black communities. As a result, the observed price decline probably reflects a significant increase in the supply of quality housing in black or in predominately black tracts.

Presumably, most of this increase stemmed from an expansion of the ghetto into areas containing large stocks of moderate quality units. The open housing legislation of the sixties, perhaps accompanied by an increased willingness on the part of realtors and banks to accept integration, may have aided this expansion process and as a result, may have dramatically increased the housing opportunities of blacks. In addition, these same factors may have tempered any previous reluctance on the part of blacks to live in racially integrated neighborhoods; if part of the premiums formerly associated with ghetto housing reflected externalities induced by a general preference of blacks to live with other blacks, this attitude appears to have changed.

Similarities in the coefficients observed in the two years prove less difficult to interpret. In both 1960 and 1970, the majority of whites appear to prefer segregated to integrated neighborhoods. In 1960, such attitudes were evidenced by the declining sector of the u-shaped curve; according to our estimates, rents in tracts that were 25 percent black were about 1.5 percent less than rents in otherwise similar all-white neighborhoods.[39] This same effect appears in 1970, where the differential between two such zones was approximately the same (1.3 percent). This negative relationship between housing prices and a tract's concentration of blacks undoubtedly reflects market externalities; in both years, the majority of whites appear to regard blacks as inferior neighbors. Although the legislation of the sixties may have ameliorated a housing shortage in established ghetto areas, its effect on the preferences of whites seems to have been negligible.

2. Proportion Italian

In both of our sample years, significant premiums were attached to Italian neighborhoods. Although it is again difficult to disentangle the effects of short-run quasi-rents, market externalities, and discriminatory markups, a brief examination of the growth and the composition of Boston's Italian community makes the case for externalities intuitively appealing. Throughout the fifties and the sixties, the Italian population consisted primarily of

---

[39] A complementary explanation views integrated tracts in a more dynamic context, where different concentrations of blacks represent different stages in a neighborhood's transition from white to black. According to this approach, a u-shaped curve would reflect a pattern of falling, then rising prices induced by the initial flight of whites and by their gradual replacement by blacks. To explore this hypothesis, tracts were divided into two mutually exclusive groups based on their proximity to established ghetto areas. Ninety-seven tracts were either within, adjacent to, or near (i.e., no more than one tract away from) the ghetto's perimeter; three hundred and thirty-nine were at least two tracts away from the fringe of the ghetto. In areas within or adjacent to the ghetto, the rent differentials exhibit a distinctly u-shaped pattern, reaching a minimum in neighborhoods that are 27 percent black. In areas beyond the path of ghetto expansion (where this dynamic interpretation is inappropriate and where no tract is more than 15 percent black), rents decline with the neighborhood's concentration of blacks reflecting the one-sided externalities of whites.

second (and third) generation Americans. According to the Census, the number of immigrants arriving in Boston between 1950 and 1970 was negligible; indeed, during the fifties, the number of first generation households actually decreased by 12 percent and during the sixties, by 15 percent. The decline and the accompanying maturation of the city's Italian community makes it unlikely that the differentials that were observed in our two samples are simply the result of housing shortages in established ethnic neighborhoods. Presumably, the majority of Italian households have the knowledge requisite to an optimal housing choice, so that informational constraints do not confine them to established Italian neighborhoods. Even if this were not the case, the stability of the Italian population over the last twenty years should have enabled the housing market to adjust to any shortages prevailing prior to 1950.[40]

On the other hand, the arguments favoring the existence of "one-sided" externalities seem particularly compelling. Strong ethnic ties within the Italian community could conceivably produce the pattern of price differentials observed in the Boston area. So long as Italians prefer living with other Italians, rents in Italian neighborhoods will be high. Numerous sociological studies have stressed the ethnic bonds uniting Italian-American communities.

---

[40] In the late 1950's, urban renewal completely destroyed the West End of Boston, a district which housed many of the city's Italian-Americans. The disequilibrating effects of this project undoubtedly placed a significant strain on Boston's stock of low to moderate quality housing, producing shortages that may have eluded the vacancy variables included in our regression. If displaced households relocated in nearby Italian districts in order to minimize the cost and the inconvenience of their move, their behavior resembled that of a new, rapidly growing migrant group and their quasi-rent argument regains its significance for the 1960 sample. However, by 1970, the disequilibrating effects of urban renewal should have disappeared.

In a study of Boston's West End, Herbert Gans documents the extreme cohesiveness of the Italian peer group and its general rejection of the greater society.[41] Such traits give rise to externalities that are capable of producing substantial price differentials in both the long and the short run. Thus, it seems reasonable to assume that a large fraction of the observed premium represents a pure neighborhood effect. Ceteris paribus, Italian households seem to prefer dwellings that are located in Italian neighborhoods.

3. Proportion Other Non-White

Prices in Chinese neighborhoods are high in both of our sample years. Although the coefficient of the variable measuring a tract's concentration of other non-whites was insignificant in the 1970 regression presented in Table 6, its unbiased estimate (Table 5) is significant and positive. Unfortunately, in this instance, a comparison of the coefficients obtained in the two years sheds little, if any light on the source of the observed differentials. In both 1960 and 1970 at least half of all individuals classified as Chinese were first generation Americans. Recent immigrants such as these may lack the knowledge requisite to an optimal housing choice and may not respond to price differentials that are inconsistent with their tastes. Thus, in the short run, housing shortages may produce significant premiums in established Chinese neighborhoods, even in the absence of market externalities.

The rapid growth of the Chinese population makes differentials of this sort entirely plausible. Between 1960 and 1970, the number of first generation Chinese-Americans increased by 80 percent. Although equivalent statistics are not available for the fifties, that decade also appears to

---

[41] Herbert Gans, The Urban Villagers (New York: Free Press of Glencoe, 1962).

have experienced a rather rapid increase in the Chinese population, since the number of individuals classified as "Other Non-Whites" grew by over 125 percent. If this rapid increase in demand produced housing shortages in these centrally located areas and if these shortages were not captured by the vacancy variable that were included in the regressions, the premiums observed in our sample may not reflect market externalities. As the Chinese increase their knowledge of the city and its housing market, and as their rate of increase declines, such differentials could presumably disappear.

4. Proportion Puerto Rican

Any interpretation of the variable reflecting a tract's concentration of Puerto Ricans encounters similar difficulties. The Puerto Rican community is relatively new to the Boston Area. Between 1960 and 1970, the number of first and second generation Americans of Puerto Rican descent increased from less than two thousand to over eleven thousand. The rapid growth of the Puerto Rican community, coupled with its relative newness to the Boston metropolitan area, establishes a strong case for short-run quasi-rents with or without market externalities. As a result, the premiums associated with Puerto Rican neighborhoods in the 1970 sample tell one very little about household preferences. Although the observed differentials could reflect externalities in the housing market, other factors may be equally important.

VI. Conclusion

This study developed a simple model of household location in order to relate demographic preferences to housing prices and housing market segregation. Under the assumptions of that model, externalities produce long-run equilibrium rent and value differentials that reflect household preferences towards the demographic mix of their neighborhood. On the surface, the empirical analysis presented in this paper supports this basic premise. In the Boston metropolitan area, significant price differentials were associated with four minority groups--blacks, Puerto Ricans, Italians, and Chinese.

However, our attempt to isolate the price effects of demographic externalities encountered several formidable obstacles. In the equations presented in this paper, the coefficients of the different demographic variables may reflect a variety of factors: market externalities, short-run quasi-rents, and perhaps discriminatory markups. On a statistical basis alone, it is impossible to distinguish between each of these three hypotheses. Nevertheless, due to the growth and the composition of two of the groups in question, it seems reasonable to attribute the source of their differentials to market externalities: the high rents in white and in Italian neighborhoods probably reflect a general preference amongst members of the two groups to live in racially and ethnically segregated neighborhoods. In the remaining two cases, our results are inconclusive.

Although the multi-faceted role of the racial and ethnic variables makes interpretation of their estimated coefficients difficult, variables of this sort undoubtedly belong in hedonic indices of housing rents and values. Past research has dealt primarily with blacks, neglecting the possibility that significant markups or discounts could be associated with other minority groups. From the size of the differentials estimated in our two samples, blacks do not appear to occupy a particularly unique position in the explanation of rents; indeed, according to our estimates, other racial and ethnic groups are equally important.

The results of the Boston analysis might easily hold for other cities in the country. Blacks, Puerto Ricans, Italians and Chinese have a number of characteristics in common: each is a readily identifiable minority group which is large enough to populate at least a few ethnic neighborhoods; each supports its own cultural institutions; and each is somewhat segregated from the greater society. If the results of this study can be generalized, one would expect significant rent differentials to be associated with similar groups in other areas of the country. In many instances, studies which include blacks as their only demographic variable may be ignoring important determinants of market prices.

Appendix I

THE UNWEIGHTED STAGE II REGRESSIONS FOR 1970

Sample	Owners	Renters
Ln (Distance)	-.1123 (4.188)	-.0809 (4.650)
Tax Rate	-.0019 (3.662)	.0010 (2.876)
Per Pupil Elementary School Expenditures ($100's)	.0373 (6.507)	.0211 (5.533)
Average Income ($1000's)	.0119 (4.292)	.0089 (4.931)
Proportion Low Status	-2.000 (9.272)	-1.375 (10.45)
Proportion Black	-.0781 (1.218)	-.0548 (1.437)
Proportion Other Non-White	1.961 (4.018)	.3598 (2.093)
Proportion Italian	.5422 (4.293)	.1096 (1.588)
Proportion Puerto Rican	-.3553 (1.040)	.2811 (1.479)
Proportion Public Housing	-.0743 (0.774)	-.3210 (5.440)
Proportion Vacant	-1.541 (3.684)	-.2473 (1.081)
Air Pollution	-3.154 (3.151)	-2.035 (3.147)
Constant	.1674 (1.585)	.0495 (0.723)
R^2	.72	.63
F	99.16	70.22
No. of Observations	480	501

Appendix II

THE 1960 AND THE 1970 STAGE I REGRESSIONS WITH NEIGHBORHOOD PROXIES

Dependent Variable	Ln(Value)	Ln(Value)	Ln(Rent)	Ln(Rent)
Sample Year	1960	1970	1960	1970
Ln (Rooms)	.46 (21.89)	.52 (21.78)	.29 (24.82)	.30 (23.49)
Central Heat	.34 (11.37)	.10 (2.642)	.23 (21.23)	.08 (5.428)
Units in Structure				
a. Duplex	.11 (3.350)	---	-.02 (1.120)	-.08 (3.505)
b. Three or More	.21 (5.420)	---	-.04 (2.750)	0.10 (4.433)
Basement	.11 (4.240)	.08 (3.178)	.03 (1.170)	.08 (3.628)
Sound Condition	.26 (11.08)	---	.06 (5.280)	---
More than One Bathroom	.30 (23.27)	.28 (21.16)	.27 (8.880)	.21 (9.204)
Age of Structure				
a. Built 1960-1970	---	.24 (12.85)	---	.23 (13.76)
b. Built 1950-1959	.28 (18.60)	.23 (14.08)	-.07 (3.600)	-.12 (6.139)
c. Built 1940-1949	.20 (10.26)	.18 (8.676)	-.11 (4.920)	-.06 (3.239)
Complete Plumbing Facilities	.21 (4.950)	.15 (2.175)	.23 (16.19)	.26 (10.56)
Crowding				
a. Less than 0.5 Persons per Room	.04 (3.550)	.03 (2.537)	-.06 (6.410)	-.04 (3.534)

Appendix II (cont'd)

b. Over 1.0 persons per Room	-.06 (2.330)	-.10 (3.520)	-.02 (0.950)	-.07 (2.795)
Length of Residency				
a. 7-20 years	-.04 (3.080)	-.08 (5.583)	-.08 (8.070)	-.15 (11.20)
b. Over 20 years	-.08 (4.810)	-.12 (6.534)	-.10 (6.940)	-.22 (10.49)
White Household Head	.12 (2.150)	.17 (3.004)	.02 (1.040)	.14 (6.933)
Central City Location	-.17 (13.81)	-.26 (11.97)	-.08 (8.470)	.00 (0.290)
Constant	7.58 (93.42)	8.44 (92.36)	3.57 (93.57)	4.07 (84.82)
R^2	.44	.45	.40	.30
F	208.75	195.91	189.97	107.97
No. of Observations	4,284	3,364	4,651	3,985

Appendix III

AN ECONOMETRIC ANALYSIS OF THE INFLUENCE OF THE STAGE I NEIGHBORHOOD PROXIES

The precise effect of adding neighborhood proxies to the Stage I equations can be determined by comparing the estimates of "b" that would be obtained if one regressed rent on both the structural and the neighborhood attributes of the unit with those obtained using a two-staged technique with proxies. The best linear unbiased estimate of "b" (obtained by regressing "R" on "X" and "N") is:

$$\tilde{b} = (N'MN)^{-1} N'MR$$

where $M = I - X(X'X)^{-1}X'$. Our Stage I regression with proxies (P) yields the following estimate of "a":

$$\hat{a} = (X'X)^{-1} X'R - (X'X)^{-1} X'P (P'MP)^{-1} P'MR$$

Regressing "$R - X\hat{a}$" on "N", we obtain our Stage II estimates of the neighborhood parameters:

$$\hat{b} = (N'N)^{-1} N' (R - X\hat{a})$$

$$= (N'N)^{-1} N'MR + (N'N)^{-1} N' X (X'X)^{-1} X'P (P'MP)^{-1} P'MR$$

$$= (N'N)^{-1} (N'MN) (N'MN)^{-1} N'MR + (N'N)^{-1} N'X (X'X)^{-1} X') (P'MP)^{-1} P'MR$$

$$= \tilde{b} + (N'N)^{-1} N'X(X'X)^{-1}X' \left[P(P'MP)^{-1}P' - N(N'MN)^{-1}N' \right] MR$$

Assuming $N'X \neq 0$, $\hat{b}$ is B. L. U. E. if and only if:

$$P(P'MP)^{-1} P' = N(N'MN)^{-1} N'$$

This last condition requires a set of proxies "P" with the following property: when each omitted neighborhood variable "N_j" is regressed on $\{X, P\}$, the estimated coefficients of the structural variables are zero. In such instances, $E(\hat{a}) = a$ and the Stage II estimates of "b" are best linear unbiased estimates of the true neighborhood parameters.

Appendix III

CALCULATION OF THE DEPENDENT VARIABLE IN THE 1970
TENURE-SPECIFIC EQUATIONS

In the owner equation, the dependent variable represents the average tract difference between the actual and the predicted logarithm of the reported value of its owner-occupied units.

$$(RES)_t^o = \frac{1}{n_{ot}} \sum_{i=1}^{n_{ot}} (\ln V_{it} - \ln \hat{V}_{it})$$

$$= \frac{1}{n_{ot}} \sum_{i=1}^{n_{ot}} \ln V_{it} - \frac{1}{n_{ot}} \sum_{i=1}^{n_{ot}} (\hat{c} + \sum_{j=1}^{14} \hat{a}_j X_{jit}^o)$$

$$= \frac{1}{n_{ot}} \sum_{i=1}^{n_{ot}} \ln V_{it} - (\hat{c} + \sum_{j=1}^{14} a_j \bar{X}_{jt}^o)$$

where "n_{ot}" is the number of owner-occupied units in the tract; "$\hat{a}_j$" is the estimated coefficient of the "j^{th}" structural (or household) attribute in the Stage I equation for owners; "$\bar{X}_j^o$" is the average value of the "j^{th}" structural (or household) variable for the owner-occupied units in the tract; and "$\hat{c}$" (=8.937) is a constant derived by inserting the average sample values of the Stage I neighborhood variables in the State I equation for owners. Note that, since the Stage I neighborhood coefficients may be subject to considerable bias, they are not used to calculate the estimated tract residuals. Instead, their average values are substituted into the regression equation, changing its constant term from .068 to 8.94.[1] The dependent variable appearing in in the renter equation has an analogous definition; predicted tract rents depend only on the structural attributes of the tract's rental units.

---

[1]This procedure reflects the relationship between constant and the average value of its omitted variables. If "X" and "N" are independent, a regression of rent on "X" alone would yield an intercept equal to the underlying constant plus the average contribution of the omitted variables (=$B\bar{N}$). (See Rao and Miller, op. cit., p. 3.)

Appendix V

MERGING TENURE GROUPS IN THE STAGE II REGRESSIONS

In the 1960 (and comparable 1970) Stage II equations, "average tract rent" is a weighted average of the gross rents of rental units and the imputed rents of owner-occupied units:

$$\ln R_t = \frac{\left[\sum_{i=1}^{n_{rt}} \ln R_{it} + \sum_{j=1}^{n_{ot}} \ln(V_{jt} \cdot r_t)\right]}{(n_{rt} + n_{ot})}$$

where:

R_{it} = rent of the "i^{th}" rental unit in the tract.

V_{jt} = value of the "j^{th}" owner-occupied unit in the tract.

r_t = calculated rent-value ratio.

n_{rt} = number of rental units in the tract.

n_{ot} = number of owner-occupied units in the tract.

The rent-value ratios ("r_t") appearing in the above equation are derived from the structural characteristics of the tracts' dwelling units, so that:

$$\ln(R/V)_t = m + \sum_{j=1}^{14} (\hat{a}_j - \hat{b}_j) \bar{X}_{jt}$$

where $\bar{X}_{jt}$ is the average value of the "j^{th}" structural attribute; $\hat{a}_j$ and $\hat{b}_j$ are the estimated coefficients of the "j^{th}" structural attribute from the Stage I renter and owner equations, respectively; and:

$$m = (\hat{a}_o - \hat{b}_o) + (\hat{a}_{15} - \hat{b}_{15}) \cdot W + (\hat{a}_{16} - \hat{b}_{16}) \cdot CC$$

where $\hat{b}_o$ is the estimated constant from the owner's equation, "$\hat{b}_{15}$" and "$\hat{b}_{16}$" are the estimated coefficients of the race and central city dummies; and $\hat{a}_o$, $\hat{a}_{15}$ and $\hat{a}_{16}$ are equivalent parameters from the Stage I equation for renters.

ADDITIONAL INSTITUTE PUBLICATIONS ON HOUSING

BOOKS AND REPORTS

New Towns-In Town: Why a Federal Program Failed, Martha Derthick, 1972, URI 70006, 102 pp., $2.95

Mobile Homes: The Unrecognized Revolution in American Housing, Margaret Drury, 1972, URI 70009, Hard cover, $15.00

Thinking About Housing: A Policy Research Agenda, Morton L. Isler, 1970, URI 60004, 47 pp., $1.25

Property Taxation, Housing and Urban Growth: With Attention to Tax Reform and Assessment Modernization, Walter Rybeck, Moderator, 1970, URI 30002, 72 pp., $2.50

Operating Costs in Public Housing: A Financial Crisis, Frank de Leeuw and Eleanor Lippman Tarutis, 1969, URI 30001, 63 pp., $1.50

PAPERS

Publicly Provided and Assisted Housing in the U.S.A.: Report on HUD's Housing Management Policies and Programs, John Macey, 1972, URI 30010, 80 pp., $1.00

The Distribution of Housing Services, Frank de Leeuw, 1972, URI 14000, 121 pp., $3.00

Residential Zoning and Equal Housing Opportunities: A Case Study in Black Jack, Missouri, Ronald F. Kirby, Frank de Leeuw, and William Silverman, assisted by Grace Dawson, 1972, URI 19000, 34 pp., $2.00

The Transfer Cost of a Housing Allowance: Conceptual Issues and Benefit Patterns, John D. Heinberg, 1971, URI 30004, 80 pp., $2.50

The Design of a Housing Allowance, Frank de Leeuw, Sam H. Leaman, and Helen Blank, 1970, URI 30005, 42 pp., $2.00

Housing Management: A Progress Report, Morton L. Isler, Margaret J. Drury, and Clay H. Wellborn, 1971, URI 30006, 106 pp., $2.50

Time Lags in the Rental Housing Market, Frank de Leeuw and Nkanta F. Ekanem, 1970, URI 80006, 57 pp., $1.50

Land Banking: Public Policy Alternatives and Dilemmas, Sylvan Kamm, 1970, URI 30007, 74 pp., $2.00

REPRINTS

The Demand for Housing: A Review of Cross-Section Evidence, Frank de Leeuw and Nkanta F. Ekanem, 1971, URI 40005, 10 pp., 50¢

The Goals of Housing Subsidy Programs, Morton L. Isler, 1971, URI 10020, 23 pp., 50¢

The Housing Allowance Approach, Frank de Leeuw, URI 10021, 15 pp., 50¢

The Incidence of Differential Property Taxes on Urban Housing: A Comment and Some Further Evidence, John D. Heinberg and Wallace E. Oates, URI 10018, 8 pp., 50¢

The Section 23 Leasing Program, Frank de Leeuw and Sam H. Leaman, 1972, URI 10087, 18 pp., 50¢

The Supply of Rental Housing, Frank de Leeuw and Nkanta F. Ekanem, 1971, URI 40009, 12 pp., 50¢

THE URBAN INSTITUTE
2100 M Street, N.W., Washington, D.C. 20037

Soc
HD
7287.5
S34